Preaching the Epistles

Raymond F. Collins

PAULIST PRESS
New York/Mahwah, N.J.

Library of Congress Cataloging-in-Publication Data

Collins, Raymond F., 1935-
   Preaching the Epistles / Raymond F. Collins.
       p.   cm.
   Includes bibliographical references and index.
   ISBN 0-8091-3625-2 (alk. paper)
   1. Bible. N.T. Epistles—Homiletical use. 2. Catholic Church—United States—Liturgy. 3. Lectionary preaching—Catholic Church. I. Title.
BS2635.5.C65   1996
251´.08—dc20   95-44467
                                                                          CIP

Published by Paulist Press
997 Macarthur Boulevard
Mahwah, New Jersey 07430

Printed and bound in the
United States of America

Contents

Foreword

For a long time I have had a strong interest in Paul, the great preacher of the faith to the Gentiles. My interest goes back to my seminary days, when my first course in New Testament was a study of the epistle to the Romans and the epistle to the Colossians. Since then, thirty-five years of priestly ministry have given me the experience of preaching in many churches, not only in my native United States, but also in a variety of English-language congregations throughout the world. My experience has been that the letters of Paul rarely serve as a basis for Sunday homilies.

What I offer here are a few reflections and suggestions as to how one might make these letters come alive for our Sunday congregations as we approach the end of the second millennium of Christianity. I offer them in honor of the apostle who was, perhaps, the greatest of all evangelists and, as Abraham Malherbe has shown so well, a true pastor, at heart and in action.[1]

I have written these reflections, not only on the basis of my pastoral experience, but also on the basis of that specific ministry to which I have been called for the past twenty-five years, namely, the interpretation of the New Testament. Had I not decided to leave this book with its simple title, I might have suggested that "An Exegete Looks at the Lectionary" serve as its subtitle. This short book has no subtitle, but I hope that the observations which follow will not only allow those who preach in the church to preach from the epistles in a more appropriate and effective manner, but that homilists and all who read herein may come to appreciate more fully the epistles in the New Testament. Its last two chapters take a closer look at how the letters of Paul and the other apostolic writings are actually used in the Sunday lectionary.

Since the Sunday homily is my principal focus, I will make ample reference to the lectionary. As I was writing the book, I had entertained the hope that the new lectionary, in keeping with the 1981 revised edition of the order of readings, would be in use in the United States at the time of its publication. Indeed, it was in anticipation of that being the case that I initially undertook this project. Fortunately I have been able to have at hand the revised New Testament of the New American Bible and the new lectionary, recently published by the Canadian Conference of Catholic Bishops. These have enabled me to take the prospective view and look at the lectionary as it will soon become available for common use in churches throughout the United States. The biblical citations in the book are, nonetheless, those of the New American Bible, as used in the 1970 Lectionary.

The book is principally directed to those who have the primary responsibility for preaching to Sunday congregations, the pastors of our parishes, but it has been written so that it might be of help to all those who exercise the ministry of preaching within the church of God. I have attempted to use inclusive language, but occasional comments reflect either my judgment on the gender of the anonymous authors of some New Testament texts or the discipline on liturgical preaching presently in force in Roman Catholicism. Hopefully, this language will not prove too much a distraction to those women of faith who, like Phoebe and Prisca, Eudoia and Syntyche, are Paul's co-workers in the ministry of evangelization.

Since this book is intended to allow the epistles to come more fully alive in the church of today, I have decided to invoke not only the anonymous homilist or nameless preacher, but also some very real congregations with which I am familiar. I beg their indulgence for having introduced them into this book, but I am convinced that preaching has very much to do with making God's word alive in the midst of very real flesh-and-blood communities. That it might become so is why I have written this book.

Raymond F. Collins

1

Food To Be Digested and Treasure To Be Shared

In many respects the most significant contribution of Vatican Council II to the life of the church today was its two dogmatic constitutions, the Dogmatic Constitution on the Church (*Lumen Gentium*), promulgated in the third session,[2] and the Dogmatic Constitution on Divine Revelation (*Dei Verbum*), promulgated during the council's fourth and final session.[3] This Constitution on Divine Revelation used two very powerful metaphors to speak of the importance of the sacred scriptures for the life of the church.

One image is food:

> The church has always venerated the divine scriptures just as she venerates the body of the Lord, since from the table of both the word of God and the body of Christ she unceasingly receives and offers to the faithful the bread of life, especially in the sacred liturgy (*Dei Verbum*, 21)[4].

> The church is concerned to move ahead daily toward a deeper understanding of the sacred scriptures so that she may unceasingly feed her children with the divine words....This task should be done in such a way that as many ministers of the divine word as possible will be able effectively to provide the nourishment of the scriptures for the people of God (*Dei Verbum*, 23).

The other is treasure:

> All ministers of the word "must share the abundant wealth of the divine word with the faithful committed to them, especially in the liturgy" (*Dei Verbum*, 25).

"The treasures of the Bible," says Vatican Council II's Constitution on the Sacred Liturgy, "are to be opened up more lavishly, so that richer fare may be provided for the faithful at the table of God's Word" (*Sacrosanctum Concilium*, 51). In like fashion, the Roman Missal reminds us: "In the readings the treasures of the Bible are opened to the people; this is the table of God's word."[5]

These powerful metaphors affirm how important the reading of the scriptures is for the life of the church. In the reading of the scriptures God's people are fed. When the scriptures are read, the treasure of God's word is opened up for them.

The council fathers recognized the importance for all the Christian faithful to experience the scriptures. "In the sacred books," they said, "the Father who is in heaven meets his children with great love and speaks with them."[6] Echoing the words of St. Jerome, they reaffirmed that "ignorance of the scriptures is ignorance of Christ."[7]

These same council fathers accorded a real pride of place to the public reading of the scriptures during the sacred liturgy. "Sacred scripture," they said, "is of paramount importance in the celebration of the liturgy" (*Sacrosanctum concilium*, 24). It is in the readings that, "God speaks to his people."[8]

It is above all through the liturgy that Christians come into contact with scripture.[9] The Pontifical Biblical Commission's document on "The Interpretation of the Bible in the Church" explains that "in principle, the liturgy…brings about the most perfect actualization of the biblical texts, for the liturgy places the proclamation in the midst of the community of believers gathered around Christ so as to draw near to God. Christ is then 'present in his word, because it is he himself who speaks when sacred scripture is read in the church.'"[10]

The Liturgical Homily

One of the reasons cited by the fathers of Vatican Council II as to why the reading of the scriptures during the liturgy is so important is that it is "from scripture that lessons are read and explained in the homily" (*Sacrosanctum concilium*, 24).

Since in the scriptures God speaks to his people, provides them with the food which they need, and offers them the treasure of his gifts, "all the preaching of the church must be nourished and ruled by sacred scripture" (*Dei Verbum*, 25).

The *General Instruction of the Roman Missal* notes that the scriptural readings form the main part of the liturgy of the word and it offers some insights into the nature of the scriptural homily. The homily "develops and completes" the liturgy of the word; it "explains the readings."

Pastorally, the function of the homily is to explain the readings. The introduction to the lectionary points to the relationship between proclamation of the word and its accompanying homiletic exposition. The lectionary speaks of the congregation's appreciation of the text "which is to be explained in the homily."[11] The 1969 Instruction on the Translation of Liturgical Texts for Celebrations with a Congregation singles out the responsibility of the homilist to explain difficult texts.[12] The homily is not simply a form of catechesis, but it does contain some element of instruction.[13]

Liturgically, the function of the homily is to actualize more explicitly the word of God, to bring about its actualization and inculturation.[14] In his classic work *The Mass*, Josef Jungmann reminded us that the task of the homily is to clothe the word in today's idiom and unfold its relevance for the men and women of today.[15] The homily is, in fact, one with the scriptures since it explains and actualizes them for the benefit of God's people, especially when they gather together for worship. From the ancient texts spiritual sustenance adapted to the present needs of the Christian community is drawn.[16] As the reading of the scriptures has been an integral part of the Christian liturgy from its earliest days, so too is the homily an integral part of the liturgy.[17] The public reading and explanation of the sacred scriptures is part of the legacy which the church has received from the Jewish community from which it takes its origin.[18]

One with the scriptures which it interprets, "the homily is to be highly esteemed as part of the liturgy itself."[19] It has, in the words of Jungmann, a mystagogical function insofar as it introduces the congregation to the celebration of the sacred mysteries and, as such, serves as the link which connects God's word with the eucharistic celebration.[20] Accordingly, said the council fathers, "at those masses which are celebrated with the assistance of the people on Sundays and feasts of obligation, it [the homily] should not be omitted except for a serious reason" (*Sacrosanctum concilium*, 52). In the life of the church the Sunday homily is especially important since it is above all during the Sunday celebration of the eucharist that Christians come into contact with the scriptures.

Suggesting norms for the celebration of the liturgy, the council fathers noted: "Since the sermon[21] is part of the liturgical service…the ministry of preaching is to be fulfilled with exactitude and fidelity. The sermon, moreover, should draw its content mainly from scriptural and liturgical sources" (*Sacrosanctum concilium*, 35). The Pontifical Biblical Commission has reminded us that the ministry of preaching is exercised especially at the close of the first part of the eucharistic celebration, in the homily which follows the proclamation of the word of God.[22]

The Table of God's Word and the Table of the Body of Christ

The eucharistic celebration brings about the most perfect actualization of the biblical texts. When the Christian community gathers to celebrate the eucharist, it gathers around two tables, the table of God's word and the table of Christ's body. From these two tables, which are ultimately but one, God's people are fed.[23]

Since the homily completes the reading of the scriptures, it completes the feeding of God's people. In the words of the introduction to the *New Order of Readings*, "the one presiding at the liturgy of the word brings the spiritual nourishment it contains to those present, especially in the homily."[24] The homily develops the treasures of God's word for the benefit of his people. The homily makes it possible for the faithful to savor the food which is offered to them; it makes it possible for them to appreciate the treasure that has been given.

In the words of the *General Instruction of the Roman Missal*, the homily is "a necessary source of nourishment of the Christian life."[25] When the faithful are deprived of a homily, they are, as it were, put on a restricted diet.[26] They are not permitted to savor the food with which they are to be nourished. When they are deprived of a homily, they are allowed only limited access to the divine treasure. They are held back from appreciating the fullness of God's beneficence.

Rights and Responsibilities

Withholding the treasure of the scriptures from God's people is an injustice. The introduction to the *New Order of Readings* explains that "the people of God have a spiritual right to receive abundantly from the treasury of God's word."[27] When the faithful are deprived of a scripturally based homily they are being deprived of one of their rights.

Since the reading and homiletic exposition of the scriptures is a matter of feeding God's people, it is clear that preaching the scriptures is a most important pastoral responsibility.[28] A shepherd must feed the flock. Preaching is, therefore, one of the principal duties of bishops, the chief pastors in the church.[29] Simon Tugwell tells the story that when Dominic de Guzman petitioned Pope Innocent III to recognize his newly founded community as the Order of Preachers, the pope was at first taken aback. He had assumed that the bishops of the church were primarily responsible for preaching God's word to his people.[30]

Priests, Vatican Council II reminds us, share in the ministry of bishops, and in their ministry of preaching.[31] Those entrusted with pastoral responsibility for a parish have a particular responsibility to preach the word of God to their people. To preach God's word is to shepherd and to govern the people. The biblical tradition proclaims that the righteous king is one who provides for those who have been entrusted to his rule. One who governs well makes the treasures which God has provided available to the people. To share the scriptures with the people of God is truly to provide for them. Hence, the importance of the homily.

At bottom, the homily is a matter of preaching the gospel. It is making the good news available to God's people; it is a matter of allowing the good news to become relevant to people in the warp and woof of their daily lives. In the homily good preachers respond specifically from the word of God and apply it to the needs and concerns of the congregation.[32]

The homily is a unique word event which allows the word of God to take root and produce fruit in those who hear it. It happens at the intersection of the word of God and the lives of his people. It occurs when the word which is proclaimed and the faith of believers come together. It is an event in which the meaning of the scriptures is unfolded anew for a specific congregation. It is a word event in which the word is enfleshed anew for the benefit of the people of God.

In most parishes today Paul's letters rarely serve as the basis of the Sunday homily.[33] This is a regrettable situation and a loss for the church. Paul's letters are an expression of the word of God. They are as much the word of God as are the canonical gospels and the books of the Old Testament. To the extent that Paul's letters are not explained to the people, to that same extent the people are deprived of some of the treasures which God has made available to them for their use. To the same extent, they are deprived of the benefit of some of the food which a loving God has provided for their nourishment.

2

The Gospel According to Paul

One of the reasons why Paul's letters do not often serve as the basis for the Sunday homily is that many people, including some clergy, have a narrow perception of "the gospel." All too often when people think about preaching the gospel, they think about preaching a homily that is based on one of the canonical gospels. They think as if "the gospel" was simply a story from one of the four canonical gospels. As a result, the appointed passage from one of the four gospels is usually the subject of the Sunday homily.

To be sure, each of the four canonical gospels is a most important expression of the good news that Jesus came to bring, the good news that was embodied in his life, ministry, and death. The good news transcends, however, any one of the four stories about Jesus that have been preserved for us from the earliest times.

Tradition has it that there is but a single gospel. There are not four gospels. There are four versions of the single gospel. Each of the "four gospels" is not the gospel. It is rather the gospel according to Matthew, the gospel according to Mark, the gospel according to Luke, or the gospel according to John. The gospel according to Matthew is Matthew's way of sharing the good news with the community for which he wrote; the gospel according to Mark, Mark's way of sharing the good news. Mark's effort was, in fact, a trail-blazing effort since he was the first Christian to write a story about Jesus.

Paul's Gospel

Paul shares the traditional Christian view that there is but one single gospel. In writing his letter to the churches of Galatia, Paul forcefully reminded his correspondents that there was ultimate-ly but one gospel (Gal 1:6-9). That one gospel is the gospel of God (1 Thess 2:9), the gospel of Christ (Gal 1:7; 1 Thess 3:2). Paul's message, even though it does not consist of stories about Jesus, is also "gospel." It, too, is the announcement of the good news of our salvation. In writing to the Romans, Paul explained his pride in the gospel which he preached. "I am," he wrote, "not ashamed of the gospel. It is the power of God for the salvation of everyone who believes" (Rom 1:16).

When Paul wrote his letters, the gospel according to Paul took on a new form. Insofar as they were Paul's way of sharing the good news with the people, his letters were written gospel. They are the written form of the gospel according to Paul.

Scripture

Paul's letters are written texts; they are scripture. In each of his letters Paul talks about "writing" (see 1 Cor 4:14; 2 Cor 1:13; Gal 1:20; Phil 3:1; 1 Thess 4:9; Phlmn 19; Rom 16:22, etc.). Insofar as Paul's letters have the obvious literary quality of being written texts, they must be considered as "scripture," that is, something which has been written.

The letters were originally intended to be read aloud to peo-ple who gathered to hear them read (see 1 Thess 5:27). The letters were Paul's proclamation in written form, but the people heard the letter as it was being read aloud. Paul's letters now belong to the canonical scriptures of our tradition, to be read to the people and explained for their benefit.

The Word of the Lord

When portions of Paul's letters are read to the congregation which gathers to celebrate the eucharistic liturgy, the reader brings the reading to closure with the acclamation, "the word of the Lord." The acclamation identifies the reading according to what it truly is, namely, the word of the Lord.

The acclamation also serves as an invitation to the congregation, asking them to respond. The response is a simple "thanks be to God." Just as Paul thanked God because the Thessalonians had received his message as the word of God (1 Thess 2:13), so now Christians thank God because they receive Paul's message as the word of God.[34]

One may look upon the reading from Paul's letters as gospel, as scripture, or as the word of the Lord. From any one of these vantage points Paul's inspired words (see 1 Cor 7:40) are words which need to be explained for the benefit of the people. Indeed, they are words which deserve to be explained, precisely because they are gospel, scripture, and the word of God.

Unfamiliar Letters

Another reason why the typical parishioner who comes to church on Sunday rarely hears the preaching of the gospel according to Paul is that many preachers are really unfamiliar with Paul's letters. Catholic preachers do not know what to make of this dynamic apostle and the sometimes strange message that his letters seem to convey.

It is no secret that the epistles of Paul, and most especially his letters to the Romans and to the Galatians, have served as the pillars of Protestant theology and have been a favorite topic for homiletic exposition within that tradition. Within Roman Catholicism it is the gospel according to Matthew which has enjoyed the position which Paul's letters have held within mainstream Protestantism.[35] Prior to the Second Vatican Council, it was passages from the gospel according to Matthew that were read most frequently on the Sundays of the church's year. When the sermon, as it was called in those days, was based on the scriptures, it was almost inevitably based on a passage of the gospel according to Matthew.

Within the Roman Catholic tradition Paul's letters do not enjoy a status similar to that which they have within the Reformed tradition. It is almost as if Catholics have handed the letters of Paul over to Protestants in order that they might be preserved within the Catholic tradition of Christianity. Since it was on the basis of Romans and Galatians that the Protestant reformation ostensibly took place, Roman Catholicism has tended to shy away from these letters, even when Catholics do not positively look askance at them. A kind of endemic ecclesial lack of familiarity with Paul's letters partially explains why they are not often the subject of homiletic exposition within Roman Catholic congregations.

The Paul of the Acts of the Apostles

A lack of familiarity with the Pauline correspondence is characteristic of most Roman Catholics. They are quite unfamiliar with Paul's letters. If they know Paul at all, it is through the medium of the Acts of the Apostles. The Paul whom they know is Paul, the legendary missionary and martyr.

Perhaps the first thing that most Catholics would have to say about Paul is that he began his missionary career on the day when he fell "from his horse" on the way to Damascus. Little are they aware that Acts has nothing to say about a Pauline journey on horseback. Neither Luke, in any of his accounts of Paul's visionary experience (Acts 9:1-19; 22:6-16; 26:12-18) nor Paul's own reflection on that event has anything to say about a ride on a horse. That so many Catholics, nonetheless, talk about Paul's career in this fashion is indicative of the amount of familiarity—that is, their real lack of familiarity!—that they have with Paul the apostle. They simply do not know Paul. Still less do they know Paul on the basis of what Paul has to say about himself.

The Rejected Paul

There is, nonetheless, an ever growing number of Roman Catholic Christians who have—or at least so they think—some familiarity with Paul. As a group these people, and especially the women among us, are inclined to reject Paul because of the things that the New Testament epistles have to say about women. These individuals tend to look upon the church as overly cautious—even restrictive—with regard to woman's role in the church and in society. They lay much of the blame for this situation squarely on the shoulders of the apostle Paul.

Reading what appears in 1 Corinthians 11:2-16 and 14:33-36, Colossians 3:18, Ephesians 5:22, 1 Timothy 2:11-15, and so forth, some people are ready to reject Paul as an unmitigated misogynist. Rejecting Paul the misogynist, they reject the only Paul whom they know. Many of these anti-Paulinists do not suspect that their "problem" is not so much the apostle Paul who actually wrote letters to various communities, especially to communities that he himself had evangelized, as it is with an image of Paul created by later tradition. Most of the passages which raise red flags for contemporary women, especially the problematic passages in Colossians, Ephesians, and 1 Timothy, were not written by the apostle himself.[36] The others must be seen within their appropriate literary and historical contexts.

The Study of the New Testament

Along with the endemic ecclesial indifference to Paul and the congregational ignorance, to which a bit of congregational antagonism can be joined, there is some real unfamiliarity with Paul on the part of those who have been appointed to preach the gospel.

Until recently, seminary courses generally offered but a single cursory overview of the Pauline letters. Catholic seminaries and theological schools have fairly up-to-date courses on the gospels, but rarely does the offering on Paul approach the quality of the courses on the synoptics and the fourth gospel. To appreciate the relative lack of professional interest in Paul, one has only to reflect on the number of good commentaries on the Pauline letters written by Roman Catholic scholars.

Many a preacher would be hard pressed to name one such commentary, except, that is, for such commentaries as are found in the single volume the *New Jerome Biblical Commentary* (1990) or its predecessor, *The Jerome Biblical Commentary* (1968). As a matter of fact, it was only in 1993 that the first major English-language commentary on the letter to the Romans written by a

Roman Catholic appeared in print. In that same year the *Etudes bibliques*, the prestigious French-language series of biblical studies which has set the pace for Roman Catholic scholarship throughout much of this century, published for the first time a commentary on the epistle to the Colossians.[37]

To compound the matter, although various homiletic programs have been developed for Roman Catholic seminaries in the past twenty years, the homiletics course frequently accepts the typical situation as a given. Seminarians are taught how to preach the gospel stories, but they are not provided with the skills which will enable them—let alone those which will motivate them!—to preach the epistles. As one veteran seminary homiletics professor put it a very few years ago, he was going to teach his students how to preach the gospels. They would never have, said he to them, any occasion to preach from the epistles.

Seminary courses in exegesis, homiletics, and spirituality make ample use of the canonical gospels, but they hardly touch upon the epistles. When Paul's letters did make their occasional way into the seminary classroom, they often appeared in the form of an isolated verse or two, served up as a standard prooftext for one or another theological thesis.

If familiarity breeds contempt, unfamiliarity may be said to breed anxiety. Many a homilist has shied away from preaching the epistles because a lack of familiarity with them has made of the unfamiliar territory an area into which he or she fears to tread. While the fear may be rational, a survey of the passages that have been chosen for incorporation into the lectionary quickly reveals that the most enigmatic and pastorally problematic passages have not made their way into the lectionary text.

An Epistle Is a Letter, Not a Story

Yet another reason why the epistles are not often the subject of the Sunday homily may be the simple fact that Paul's writings come in the form of letters. Apart from the passion narrative— but, in reality, even there!—the four classic versions of the gospel are collections of short stories about Jesus. Each of them is readily isolable from its biblical context. Each of them gets off to a clear start and is just as clearly brought to closure. Each of the gospel pericopes, in other words, makes sense in and of itself. This is not the situation when we read excerpts from Paul's letters on Sunday. A letter is not like a short story. It does not consist of a series of episodes which are narrated one after the other until the entire plot is unfolded.

When a preacher takes a gospel passage as the basis for the homily, he or she can take advantage of the fact that the individual episodes are isolable from the whole. These individual gospel pericopes had, in fact, been passed along within the early tradition as independent narratives until such time as Mark wove some of them together into that longer story which we now call the gospel according to Mark.

Each of the gospel stories about Jesus is, moreover, a story that has already been preached. The gospel according to Mark, the earliest of the four, is a collection of stories that have been handed down in the oral tradition. What Mark contains is a record of the preaching of the early church. When a contemporary homilist preaches from the gospel according to Mark, or from one of the later gospels, he or she is actually taking a good story out of a very old anthology of short stories and then retelling it with a new twist for a contemporary audience. Homiletic practice in that regard has some similarity with the situation of someone who has heard a good after-dinner story, remembers it, and then tells it again with a new twist when the occasion so warrants.

When the homilist prepares a homily based on the gospel, he or she generally assumes that the congregation is familiar with the narrative plot of the story about Jesus. The congregation may not be specifically attuned to the particular way that the plot is turned in any specific one of the four gospels, its members may not be familiar with the details specific to each of the four stories, but each member of the congregation can generally be presumed to know something of the story about Jesus. This gives the congregation ready access into the hermeneutical circle, for knowledge of the whole helps to explain its several parts. Unfortunately a homilist cannot presume that the congregation is familiar with the general thrust of any one of Paul's letters.

The Quantity of Letters

Since the reading of "the Sunday gospel" is always taken from one of the four canonical gospels, it is relatively easy for both the homilist and the congregation to get to know something about the origin and principal ideas of each of these four gospels. That the synoptic gospels are read according to a three-year plan makes it very easy for the preacher to become familiar with each of them. No major effort is required of the homilist who is willing to take the time to do so, to again become familiar with Matthew in Year A, Mark in Year B, and Luke in Year C. It proves to be not so much more difficult for the homilist to refamiliarize himself or herself with the fourth gospel during each Easter season.

Rare is the congregation which is familiar with the different biblical books from which the other Sunday readings are taken. Hardly do they appreciate the letters from which the second Sunday reading is generally taken. One might even suggest that it is the rare homilist who is familiar with these letters. Not only has the Roman Catholic experience of the past several centuries not been particularly keen on these letters, there is also the sheer quantity of the letters. There are only four canonical gospels. There are fourteen epistles in the Pauline corpus, seven Catholic epistles, and the book of Revelation—a total of twenty-two books of scripture from which readings from the apostolic writings are taken, not to mention the Acts of the Apostles which provides the text for the first scriptural reading on the Sundays of the Easter season.

These twenty-two books, and even the fourteen epistles of Paul, have much in common, but they do not share a similar plot as do the four canonical gospels. Unlike the canonical gospels whose literary interdependency is easily recognized, each of the various epistles has an identity unto itself alone.[38]

A Single Act of Communication

Passages from the letters are, moreover, not as readily isolable from their immediate literary context as are passages from the gospels. By its very nature a letter is a single act of communication; it does not consist of a series of episodes. Because the letter is a single act of communication, what an author has written in any one section can only be truly understood in the light of what has been previously written and what will be written immediately thereafter.

Thus, readings from the apostolic writings often strike the congregation as bolts from the blue. They start abruptly and end just as abruptly. The congregation's experience of the disjointedness of the reading stems from the fact that passages from the letters have been taken out of the context to which they belong.

The Epistolary Situation

Not only have these passages been taken from their literary context; that literary context is a letter. It is a well-known fact that letters presume much more than what they actually say. This is because those who write letters and those who receive them share experiences in common. Each of us has probably written a letter in which we have said something like "I had a great time Saturday afternoon." Presumably the person to whom the letter is sent knows what we are talking about, but a reader of the letter who has not shared our common experience would not really know what happened on that great Saturday afternoon.

By its very nature a letter is an ad hoc composition. Specialists in the field speak of letters as occasional compositions. All literary works arise from the circumstances in which they have been composed. This is all the more true in the case of letters. They have been written by an author to specific recipients in self-conscious response to given sets of circumstances. Thus the letter is self-consciously tied to the set of circumstances in which it has been written. This means that the liturgical readings from the apostolic writings have not only been taken from their literary context, but that their literary context is a situational one. Passages from the letters can only be understood in the light of the circumstances in which they have been written. Students of Paul know well that even very serious study of any one of the letters is not always satisfying. Often the set of circumstances in which Paul is writing can be gleaned only from his letters. Again, by their very nature letters presume more than they actually say.

The scholar's attempt to understand Paul's letters may be compared to the much easier effort that needs be made when one tries to understand a telephone conversation after hearing only one part of the conversation. One who overhears part of a conversation suffers from a real liability in trying to understand the dialogue. The hearer has to make an educated guess as to whom the unheard interlocutor is. Often, he or she has to imagine what situation has prompted the telephone call. In any case, he or she can only guess what the person on the other end of the line is saying.

One who overhears a telephone conversation has, nonetheless, a double advantage over those who try to understand an ancient letter. The one who overhears a conversation has the advantage of some non-verbals (the tone of voice, posture and mien of the one whose conversation has been heard) as well as a familiarity with the language employed and the general circumstances of the times. What an easy task of interpretation this is in comparison with trying to understand a passage that has been abruptly taken from an old letter!

Hymns, Creeds and Topoi

To be sure, occasional passages within Paul's letters are somewhat isolable from his letters. Sometimes, for example, Paul used a hymn that the tradition had independently passed along. When biblical scholars write about the hymns of scripture, they are generally not referring to hymns that have been composed for congregational singing. In terms of their form, but certainly not of their content, they are comparable to some of our well-known nursery rhymes. Biblical hymns are self-contained and generally previously composed units of material. They have not necessarily been composed by the author of the text in which they presently appear. They are characterized by distinctive vocabulary and rhythmical cadence. Thus they have been easily retained and passed along from one person to another.

One of the most significant hymns that Paul has used is the

hymn that appears in Philippians 2:6-11. This Christological hymn has been chosen as the reading from the apostolic writings on Palm Sunday. Because it is a hymn, it is readily isolable from its epistolary context. It did, after all, enjoy an independent existence before it was incorporated into Paul's letter.

On other occasions Paul makes use of credal formulas which the young tradition had previously passed along. Paul exploits one of these credal formulas in his first letter to the Corinthians (1 Cor 15:3-8). That credal formula is rehearsed, in semi-isolation, as the shortened form of the second reading appointed for the fifth Sunday of Year C. The isolation of that short formulation of traditional Christian belief is broken only insofar as the lectionary reading shares with today's congregation Paul's own introduction to the credal formula and a one-line summary of the implications which he draws from it. Something similar may be said apropos Romans 1:1-7, a passage which bears some of the characteristics of an early Christian creed and is used as a scriptural reading on the fourth Sunday in Advent (Year A).

In Paul's letters we sometimes meet a variety of topoi, that is, stock rhetorical themes or topics. These, too, can be isolated from their epistolary contexts, even though they sometimes express the very gist of Paul's letter. Such would be the case of the passage on the parousia, the future coming of Jesus as Lord, which appears in 1 Thessalonians 4:13-18. This passage serves as the liturgical reading from the apostolic writings appointed for the thirty-second Sunday of Year A.

Thus, although the typical member of the Sunday congregation has an experience of discontinuity upon hearing Paul's letters, the discontinuity is not always as pronounced as it would have been had Paul not composed his letters as he did. That he did occasionally make use of traditional material makes it just a little less difficult for today's listener to understand what Paul wrote.

Changing the Subject

When one writes letters, one frequently changes topics along the way. Paul, too, wrote in this fashion. Nowhere is this more apparent than in his first letter to the Corinthians. In this letter the apostle responds to a letter which he had received from some people within the community at Corinth (1 Cor 7:1). In the second part of his response, Paul takes up, one by one, some of the topics mentioned by the Corinthians. Paul introduces each new topic with a telltale "now concerning" (1 Cor 7:1; 7:25; 8:1; 12:1; 16:1; 16:12).

None of these formally introduced change-of-topics from 1 Corinthians has made its way into the Sunday lectionary. "Now concerning" is, however, not the only expression which Paul uses to indicate that he is moving on to another topic in his letters. He uses a variety of techniques to indicate that he is changing the subject. Some passages with a thus formally marked new beginning do appear in our lectionary. For example, an apostrophic "brothers and sisters" marks a new start in the final paraenesis of Paul's letter to the Philippians (Phil 3:17). That new beginning is the start of the lection on the second Sunday of Lent (Year C).

A Challenge for the Homilist

In sum, while there are undoubtedly difficulties in reading selections from Paul's letters when they are taken from their setting within the letters, the problems are not insurmountable. In many cases Paul himself has indicated that the passages in question were originally independent units of tradition that he has incorporated into his letters. In other cases, a clear shift in the flow of Paul's thought indicates that he has taken up another point or that he is moving on to some other point in his development.

Notwithstanding this mitigation of the difficulty of taking Paul's words out of their context, there remains the fact that letters are one-time compositions, whereas the gospel pericopes are, by and large, short stories that had been preached prior to the composition of Mark's written gospel. They are short stories that continue to be preached in our day.

In a sense a gospel pericope that contains a short story about Jesus may be compared to a frame in a motion picture. One may concentrate on the frame, but there is something artificial about concentrating on the frame. A single frame is but a single moment in an ongoing and dynamic process. So it is with the gospel pericopes. The process is the telling of the story about Jesus. A pericope in any one of the gospels does not really make the story timeless; rather, it captures the story at a single moment in the history of its tradition.

In contrast, the letters of Paul were ad hoc compositions. They were literary creations composed for the occasion; their author had no idea that they would continue to be read after he had communicated his ideas to the community to which he was writing. To continue with an analogy taken from the world of photography, we might say that the letters are like still shots. They may be well composed, but the situation which they capture happened but once. It is not a story that is kept alive in the retelling of it.

The fact that the passages from the apostolic writings chosen for liturgical reading have been extracted from their literary and historical contexts makes it difficult for a homilist to preach on these texts. This difficulty is experienced not only when the passages at hand are passages from the letters of Paul, it is also experienced when the lector reads from the book of Revelation on six successive Sundays in year C or when passages from the letter to the Hebrews are chosen for Year B and Year C.

Revelation and Hebrews

Since the topic of this book is preaching the epistles, I will defer until Chapter 5 any real discussion of the challenge of preaching from the book of Revelation. The passages taken from the letter to the Hebrews are, nonetheless, of some concern, particularly insofar as there is a semi-continuous reading from Hebrews on eight Sundays in Year B and another semicontinuous reading from the letter on four Sundays in Year C.

The so-called letter to the Hebrews is, in fact, not a letter at all. Although it has an epistolary postscript (Heb 13:22-25), the postscript may have been added when the completed literary composition was sent along. By its own admission, the so-called letter is not a letter; it is, as the text itself indicates, a "message of encouragement" (Heb 13:22). A "message" (*logos*) is a discourse or spoken address. We should look upon the letter to the Hebrews as a written homily, to which an epistolary postscript has been added (Heb 13:22-25).[39]

As a single unit of discourse, the epistle to the Hebrews is a tightly knit literary composition. The author's thought moves from homiletic exposition to hortatory exhortation. The entire essay is a well-integrated literary effort. The author develops his thought in subtle fashion, further developing themes that the readers have already heard and preparing the way for development yet to come.

Since the thought of the epistle to the Hebrews is so refined and since the pieces of the essay interlock as tightly with each other as they do, it is most difficult to take a passage out of the letter to the Hebrews and then base a sermon on it. The effort involved is akin to taking a two minute segment out of a long speech and then trying to develop the significance of that segment for the benefit of those who are otherwise unfamiliar with the speech and with the circumstances in which it had been delivered.

3

Mail for the People of God: Adapting Paul's Concerns for Today

Despite the difficulties experienced by preacher and congregation alike in dealing with the gospel according to Paul—and we must not forget that many of the potential difficulties have been removed from the "lectionary text" of the letters!—something is truly lost when these scriptures are not explained to the people. They have been put on a restricted diet, sometimes even without knowing that they have been put on a diet. They have been deprived of some part of God's gift to them.

Advantages in Preaching the Epistles

That God's people should be so deprived is regrettable, especially when we consider not only that the epistles are part of scripture, but also that they are part of scripture in the form of a letter. There is something about a letter which makes it particularly appropriate as a basis for a preacher who wishes to share, in the form of a homily, reflections on the word of God with a local congregation.

A Particular Congregation

First of all, the letters of Paul were written to specific congregations. When one reads, as one does on the twenty-ninth Sunday of the year (Year A), "Paul, Silvanus and Timothy to the church of Thessalonians in God the Father and the Lord Jesus Christ" (1 Thess 1:1), one should realize that the letter was first heard by a relatively small group of Christians, perhaps twenty or thirty, who had gathered together in someone's home. Now a new group of Christians, those who have gathered in St. Lucy's in Middletown or St. Joseph's in Grand Junction, for instance, are similarly listening to the reading of Paul's letter.

The contemporary congregation is undoubtedly larger than the gathering at Thessalonica, but it has come together, like the Christians at Thessalonica, to listen to the reading of Paul's letter.[40] The entire population of Thessalonica did not get together to listen to the message which had been sent by the apostle. It was only those chosen by God who came together to listen to the reading of the letter from Paul and his friends. Similarly today it is only God's chosen people who gather in order to listen to a reading from Paul's letter. Not all the people who live in Middletown or Grand Junction gather on a day in the late fall, on the twenty-ninth Sunday of the year, to listen to Paul speaking about the significance of the Thessalonians having been chosen by God (1 Thess 1:4). Just some of the people in Middletown or Grand Junction—those whom God has chosen—come to church to listen to the reading of Paul's words.

The reading of the beginning of the letter to the Thessalonians provides a marvelous occasion for a homilist to reflect on the church. One of several tacks may be taken, each of them potentially very rich. For Paul, the church is essentially the local church. In his language, "church" (*ekklēsia*) means "a gathering." The church is a gathering. The "church" is not so much the church in general as it is the people who have actually come together in Middletown and those who have actually assembled in Grand Junction. The church is a group of people who have gathered to hear God's word. The church is a group of people for whom the scriptures have been written. The church is a group of people who have been chosen by God. The church is a group of people who belong to God the Father and the Lord Jesus Christ.[41] A group of such people had gathered together long ago in Thessalonica; now a group of such people are gathering together in Middletown and Grand Junction.

Homilists often seek an occasion to reflect on the nature of the church. The reading of the beginning of Paul's first letter to the Thessalonians on a twenty-ninth Sunday of the year presents an opportune occasion for doing so.

Practical Matters

The letters are not only congregation-specific, they also deal with real issues. Many a church leader occasionally experiences the need to forego a homily in order to give an instruction or to preach a sermon (as distinct from a homily) on some issue that is of particular moment. Foregoing the scriptural homily in these circumstances may be a wise and responsible pastoral decision. It is a decision which should be made by way of exception, since it is the pastor's primary responsibility to preach the word of God to his people. There are, however, extraordinary or particularly urgent situations that require this kind of pastoral decision.

A wise pastor should, nonetheless, realize what has been done. Hopefully, the congregation will also realize what has been done. What has happened is that, for presumably good pastoral reasons, a decision has been made to omit the homily[42] and to replace it with a sermon or an instruction on one or another topic. What has been lost is an opportunity to explain the scriptures for the nourishment of God's people. What has happened is that one has decided not to follow the liturgical directives and the conciliar instructions.

Money, for One

One of the things that many pastors do not like to talk about is money. Often they feel ill at ease when they deem it necessary to forego the homily in order to talk about money. Money is, nonetheless, a fact of life. People need money in order to live; groups of people need money in order to survive. A church must raise sufficient funds if it is to meet its basic needs and fulfill its mission.

Because of their personal temperament, their theological con-
victions, or their pastoral strategies, many pastors assign the
"money talk" to members of the parish finance committee. In
and of itself this may be a good thing. It is usually good pastoral
strategy to handle money matters in this way. The price to be
paid, however, is usually the sacrifice of a scripturally-based
homily for the day. A message is also conveyed when the only
time that a lay person is seen in the pulpit is on the occasion of a
money talk. The medium is the message! The message is that the
laity are competent where money is concerned, but they are
incompetent to testify to their faith. The occasion of this book is
not the occasion to entertain a useful, and increasingly necessary,
discussion about the competency of the laity to preach nor a discussion about when and where the laity might appropriately
preach.[43] The occasion of this book does, however, provide an
opportunity to recall that in his letters Paul dealt with many day-
to-day matters facing his congregations.

The pastor of the church of the Holy Spirit in Memphis is not
the only pastor who has ever experienced a need to talk about
money. Paul, the pastor, did so. In each of his four longest letters,
Romans, 1 and 2 Corinthians and Galatians, he wrote about the
collection for the saints.[44] As a matter of fact, in each of the
authentic letters, Paul presents himself in some way as being
engaged in a financial transaction on behalf of his mission.[45]

People do not like to hear about collections. Modern-day congregations are not unique in this regard. The Christians of Corinth
also had some questions about money. A money matter was one of
the things about which they wrote to Paul in the letter to which 1
Corinthians was the response (see 1 Cor 16:1-4).

The lectionary is sparing in its selection of passages in which
Paul deals with money matters. Money matters seem to be one of
those difficult matters which the lectionary seeks to avoid. Its
asceticism in this regard serves as an indication as to how the
church presently views its mission of sharing God's word with
the people. The lectionary does, however, provide for the reading
of 2 Corinthians 8:7, 9, 13-15 on the thirteenth Sunday of the year
(Year B). Had the lectionary not provided such a reading, the lec-

tionary text would have prevented the typical Sunday congregation from having a full picture of Paul the pastor at work.

The passage from 2 Corinthians, extracted from a long section on the collection (2 Corinthians 8—9), recalls that "your surplus at the present time should supply their needs, so that their surplus may also supply your needs, that there may be equality." What an occasion for a scripturally-based "money talk"! What an opportunity to reflect on social justice or the new economic order within the context of a Sunday homily!

The lectionary provides an occasion for the homilist to really preach about such practical matters. On this occasion, the homily would be appropriate and scripturally grounded. It would have an excellent theological foundation. Paul reminded the Christians at Corinth, as he reminds those who listen to his words today, that the Lord Jesus Christ became poor for our sake so that by his poverty we might become rich (2 Cor 8:9).

The preacher who is truly sensitive to what Paul has written might recall that Paul's description of Jesus as Lord is not entirely accidental. True, "Lord" is Paul's favorite way of referring to Christ, but in this passage it is especially meaningful. A lord, after all, was a land owner (we still commonly speak of the lord of the manor!). The lord was one who controlled the lives of those who worked the land. When Paul calls Jesus "Lord" in 1 Corinthians 8, he recalls that the Lord Jesus is one who possesses all things. The lord has authority. Those who are under that authority are expected to respond appropriately.

Sex, death and money are matters of concern for every human being. They are, nonetheless, topics which even married couples find it difficult to converse about. They are matters about which preachers find it difficult to preach. Yet every pastor knows how important it is that Christians have a Christian attitude with regard to sex, death, and money.

Sex, death, and money, these three, are but a few of the very practical matters that Paul addresses in his various letters. He was well aware that real faith was not so much veneer on one's life. The life of faith goes beyond the congregation's gathering together. Real faith touches life in the depth and in the practicality of it. Thus Paul wrote about faith as it touched upon sex, death, and money. Is it not appropriate for today's homilist to facilitate the congregation's embodiment of the faith by reflecting homiletically upon such matters as sex, death, and money?

Sex, death, and money were not, of course, the only practical issues with which Paul dealt in his letters. He also wrote about tensions in the community, authority, the ten commandments, love, women, new movements of the spirit, and the like. When preachers experience a need to give practical instruction or moral exhortation, rather than foregoing the homily for the sake of the instruction or admonition, it might be better for them to turn to Paul and preach a homily on the basis of one of his letters. His letters, after all, clearly reveal that the Christian message affects people exactly where they are at.

Updating the Message

One of the purposes of a homily is to make the scriptures relevant to the community which has listened to the reading of the sacred text. "Pastors," says the Introduction to the *New Order of Readings*,[46] "may wish to respond specifically from the word of God to the concerns of their own congregation."

A good homily allows the scriptures to be part of the living tradition of the church at the present time. On the practical level, this requires that the homilist discern the analogy between the situation of the congregation and that of those to whom the biblical text was originally addressed.

The homilist should be aware that this way of approaching the scriptures of the New Testament is consistent with the New Testament witness itself. Students of the synoptic gospels are well aware that most scholars are now convinced that Mark is the earliest of these three gospels. Matthew and Luke were written at a later time and in dependence on Mark. The gospel according to Matthew and the gospel according to Luke are really two distinct revised and expanded editions of the Markan text. The revisions were made in accordance with the respective needs of the Matthean and Lukan communities and in keeping with the theological insights and literary skills of the respective evangelists. When a homilist brings the situation of the community to bear upon the biblical text, he or she is continuing to do the work that Matthew and Luke did in their own times and in their own way.

The situation is somewhat different when one preaches from the gospel according to Paul. His letters are, as has been noted, one-time acts of communication. Because they are letters rather than a short story, there is no new and revised edition as there is in the case of the gospel according to Mark. Nevertheless, the early Christian churches evangelized by Paul did experience the need to adapt the Pauline tradition to their own new and particular circumstances. It was out of this need that the deutero-Pauline literature was born.

In the late first century it was a common enough practice for people to write "letters" in another's name. Sometimes duplicity or malicious intent was involved in the writing of these pseudepigraphal writings. In other cases, however, the writing of such a letter was a way of paying honor to a revered figure. Thus it came to pass that after the death of Paul the apostle, some of his disciples wrote letters in his name.

Today most biblical scholars are of the opinion that six letters in the New Testament's Pauline collection were not actually written by the apostle.[47] These six are the epistle to the Ephesians, the epistle to the Colossians, the second epistle to the Thessalonians, the two letters to Timothy, and the letter to Titus.[48] While the epistles to the Ephesians, the Colossians, the Thessalonians (2 Thessalonians), Timothy, and Titus appear to be letters, they are not really letters. They are literary essays which have appropriated the apostle's manner of composition. Their common purpose was to actualize the Pauline tradition, that is, to adapt it to a new era and a new set of circumstances.

The New Testament's collection of deutero-Pauline letters includes two texts that have something of the character of a new and revised edition. These are the second letter to the Thessalonians and the letter to the Ephesians.

2 Thessalonians

In the letter which Paul wrote to the Thessalonians [= 1 Thessalonians], he spoke about the kingdom and the coming of Jesus as Lord. Paul wrote as if the eschatological event was to occur at any moment. He wrote as if he expected the parousia to occur during his own lifetime (1 Thess 4:15, 17). The parousia, as Paul awaited it with eager expectation, did not occur in Paul's lifetime. It has not yet occurred in ours. Indeed, apart from a few apocalyptic Christians, there are few believers today who expect the kingdom of God to arrive in our century.

The expectation of an imminent parousia was beginning to wane while Paul was still alive. The kind of apocalyptic excitement that is manifest in his early letters, that is, in his correspondence with the Thessalonians and the Corinthians, seems to be absent from his later letters. As the years went on, the expectation of an imminent parousia continued to lessen in intensity. By the time that Jerusalem had been destroyed and the temple razed in 70 A.D., some few years after Paul's death, Christians had begun to accommodate their thinking to the idea that the Christian movement, with its gatherings of people in various house churches throughout the empire, was here to stay.

The new situation prompted an unknown disciple of Paul to rewrite, as it were, Paul's letter to the Thessalonians [1 Thessalonians]. The rewriting was a way of maintaining the authority of the apostle for Christians who had seen Paul die before the parousia occurred. Some scholars think that this new edition was intended to be read in addition to Paul's own letter, so that the apostolic tradition would appear to be modified by Paul's recasting of his apocalyptic teaching. Another, and somewhat more radical, group of scholars think that the author of the second letter to the Thessalonians intended that the new composition should replace the letter that Paul had written.

In either event, the second letter to the Thessalonians was written in order to modify the understanding of Paul's apocalyptic thought. It revised what the apostle had to say about the coming of the Lord Jesus Christ in such a way that Paul's apostolic authority was maintained in a new set of circumstances. In this new version of Paul's vision, the image of Jesus as eschato-logical Lord is maintained, but the figure of the parousiac Lord has been recast (compare 1 Thess 4:13-18 and 2 Thess 2:1-12, for example). According to the new version an entire sequence of events, as yet mysterious, is expected to occur before Jesus will come as parousiac Lord. In 2 Thessalonians, moreover, the func-tion of Jesus as eschatological Lord is focused much more on his role as judge of the present age than it was in 1 Thessalonians.

Ephesians

Among the epistles, that to the Ephesians is very special. Its singular importance is reflected by the lectionary which—despite the relative brevity of this text—has selected eight pas-sages for a semi-continuous reading in Year B. The lectionary has also assigned other passages from the epistle to the Ephesians to be read on the second Sunday after Christmas, the feast of the Epiphany and the feast of the Ascension in all three years of the liturgical cycle. Proportionately, no other apostolic writing is read as intensely during the church's celebration of its Sunday eucharist as is the epistle to the Ephesians.

The epistle to the Ephesians is also very special insofar as the thought of the epistle is carefully developed. The church univer-sal is its principal theme. The picture is a well-manicured por-trait. In flowing phrases and with graphic imagery, the epistle presents a picture of the universal church with Christ as its head. The text is so well put together that the epistle seems to be more of a theological meditation than a person-to-person(s) letter. One could almost call it the church's first treatise on ecclesiology.

That precisely is the rub. Paul stayed with the Ephesians for about three years. The epistle to the Ephesians exudes, however, none of the warmth and friendly tone that one might expect from Paul who had lived so long in a community in which he had such good friends and business partners as Prisca and Aquila. In all of his letters Paul writes about the church, but his "church" is a local community, a gathering at home. The "church" of the

Ephesians is, in contrast, the universal church, the single body of Christ.

When Paul wrote letters, his style was that of a person on the move. His letters reflect the style of a person who is responding to the situation at hand. The style of the epistle to the Ephesians, however, is heavy and ponderous. It evinces none of the impulse which seems to have driven Paul the apostle, a true man of letters. It lacks even the friendly "brothers and sisters" which punctuates the letters to the communities beloved by Paul (see 1 Corinthians, Philippians, 1 Thessalonians).

In the sixteenth century, Erasmus of Rotterdam, the great humanist, remarked that the style of the epistle to the Ephesians could appear to be that of someone other than the apostle Paul. Since the beginning of the nineteenth century scholars have been increasingly of the opinion that the epistle to the Ephesians was not written by Paul. Some of these scholars have suggested that Ephesians might have been written as a companion piece to Paul's letters at the time that they were collected together and began to circulate, as a collection, among some of the early Christian churches.

When the epistle to the Ephesians is compared with the epistle to the Colossians—a text much less emphasized by the lectionary than the text of Ephesians—it appears that Ephesians is somehow dependent on the earlier and shorter epistle to the Colossians. Its style and more developed theology suggest that Ephesians is virtually the result of a rewriting of the epistle to the Colossians.[49] This is another reason for thinking that the epistle to the Ephesians was probably not written by Paul himself.

The Pauline Pseudepigrapha

When a homilist preaches from the letters attributed to Paul, but not actually written by him, he or she is following in the tradition created by the anonymous authors of the New Testament's pseudepigraphal letters. The preacher is doing what they did—adapting the apostolic tradition to the circumstances of a later time. Since the tradition is ultimately a living one, it is best preserved by being adapted to new circumstances.

When a homilist preaches a true homily on any one of these deutero-Pauline texts and allows the word of God to overshadow personal skills and flair, he or she is doing what the anonymous authors of our tradition have done. Choosing anonymity was their way to allow respect for the Pauline tradition to dominate over their personal contribution to the text which they had written.

The Author of These Epistles

When preaching from these epistles, that is from Ephesians, Colossians, 2 Thessalonians, 1 and 2 Timothy, and Titus, the homilist is immediately confronted by a problem. How does one talk about the anonymous author of these texts? What language is appropriate to describe the unknown person who wrote epistles in the name of Paul the apostle?

The homily is not the appropriate means for instructing the faithful on the criteria for judging an epistle to be pseudepigraphal. The pulpit is not the place for that kind of exegesis. That kind of instruction belongs in the classroom. It can be given in an adult education session or in the context of bible study, but it ought not to be given in a homily. The homily is a kind of communication which is quite different from the classroom lecture or interactive classroom discussion. A preacher should not substitute a class in New Testament exegesis for the homily.

On the other hand, a good and pastorally sensitive homily should not continue to reinforce a traditional idea which critical scholarship overwhelmingly judges to be wrong. While preaching from these pseudepigraphal texts, the homilist who is aware of contemporary scholarly opinion about the authorship of these texts will find appropriate ways to speak about the one who wrote Ephesians, Colossians, 2 Thessalonians, and the pastoral epistles. The preacher might refer to "the author" or "the writer." Alternatively, reference can be made to what "the text says" or what "the disciple of Paul has written."

Over and over again my pastoral experience has shown just how significant this way of addressing the issue truly is. On many occasions, after I have preached on one of the epistles that Paul really did not write, different members of the congregation have asked me why it was that I mentioned only the "author" and never spoke about St. Paul. Their question gave me, even on the steps of the church, occasion to address the issue in a personal and significant fashion. Sometimes it led to an adult education session at which I could talk about the letters that Paul did not write, about the significance of pseudepigraphy in the early days of the church, and about what it means for the church of today.

As a result of some of these conversations, or as a result of occasional classroom discussions, I have heard readers begin the liturgical reading of a passage from one of the letters that Paul did not write with a simple "A reading from the epistle to the Ephesians." People tend to pay attention when a liturgical reading is introduced in this fashion. As a result, the discussion continues and people's appreciation of the New Testament scriptures continues to grow.

In this regard, it may be interesting to note that the 1970 English-language lectionary[50] continues to use "a reading from the letter of Paul to the Hebrews" as the introduction to the scriptural lection on Christmas Day and on Good Friday, but employs a more simple form, namely, "a reading from the letter to the Hebrews," when Hebrews is read in semicontinuous fashion on the Sundays of Years B and C and the weekdays of Year I. The introduction to the *New Order of Readings* states that the inscription should be "the Letter to the Hebrews,"[51] with no mention of Paul.

Tradition

Preaching from the letters attributed to, but not actually written by, Paul gives the homilist the opportunity to preach about tradition in the life of the church. "Tradition," wrote Jaroslav Pelikan, "is the living faith of the dead; traditionalism is the dead faith of the living." The existence of the deutero-Pauline letters is a canonical example of the church, in its formative and normative period, taking the apostolic witness and keeping it alive by actualizing it for a new day.

The Twenty-Seventh Sunday of the Year (Year C)

A fine opportunity for reflecting on tradition, and the function of the deutero-Pauline letters as a witness to the living tradition of the church, might well be the twenty-seventh Sunday in the year (Year C). On that day the reading from the apostolic writings is taken from the second letter to Timothy (2 Tim 1:6-8, 13-14).

According to the New American Bible [NAB] and the 1970 lectionary based on it, 2 Timothy 1:14 mentions "the rich deposit of faith." "Of faith" is not found in the Greek text, nor is it in the Latin Vulgate, which renders the Greek *kalē parathēkē* as *depositum*. It is, however, this translation which is reflected in the traditional formulation, "the deposit of faith" *(depositum fidei)*. The New Revised Standard Version of the Bible [NRSV] reads the Greek expression as "the good treasure entrusted to you," while the revised New American Bible offers "this rich trust" as its translation. The biblical text (v. 14) remarks not only that the treasure must be preserved but that this is to be done "with the help of the Holy Spirit that dwells within us."

Earlier in the passage to be read on the twenty-seventh Sunday of the year, mention was made of the "sound words which you have heard from me" (v. 13). "Sound words" is a formula which echoes throughout the pastoral epistles. It conjures up notions of the validity and utility of the teaching which is endorsed with this "seal of approval." Within the pastorals themselves, the expression proclaims that the traditional teaching is correct and truly beneficial for the audience.

The expression "which you have heard from me" gives any preacher an occasion to reflect on how the teaching of Paul has been passed along in the church. This reflection provides the skillful homilist with an opportunity to instruct the congregation that the pastoral epistles—and the other deutero-Paulines, one might add—are themselves an expression of the handing down of the tradition, that is, of a tradition whose roots lay some time in the past, in that time when Paul actually preached and wrote his letters.

The reading from 2 Timothy on the twenty-seventh Sunday of the year clearly provides the homilist with an occasion for preaching about the living tradition of the church and the role of the deutero-Paulines therein. These are matters about which any congregation might be profitably instructed. The people of St. Peter's in Fort Worth should understand how tradition functions in the church, how tradition functions by calling those in the present to be faithful to the past in an way which is ever so contemporary. While the reading assigned to the twenty-seventh Sunday of the year is ready-made for such a homiletic reflection, other passages from the deutero-Paulines provide similar opportunities.

4

Talking About Someone Else's Mail: Preaching Year A of the Lectionary

Since three scriptural readings have been introduced into the celebration of the Sunday eucharist and these readings have been distributed over a three year cycle so that the faithful might be more fully exposed to the word of God, it is good pastoral practice for homilists to capitalize on each of these scriptures.

Otherwise, the faithful might get the impression that the reading of some of these texts, especially the reading of the letters of Paul, is merely a liturgical exercise which must be done in order to satisfy the requirements of liturgical law. Pertinent homilies implicitly teach the faithful about the importance of these texts within the liturgy, while they explicitly explain the significance of the texts for Christian life and faith.

That passages from the letters of Paul and other apostolic writings have been chosen on the basis of the principle of semicontinuous reading means that, in principle, they do not enjoy thematic harmony with the first and third readings of the day. The homilist who develops the homily on the basis of the scriptural readings must therefore make a decision. The homily should be based either on the thematically related first and third readings or on the independent second reading. A good homilist must make a choice between preaching the Jewish scriptures and the "gospel" and preaching the second reading of the day.

It is poor homiletic practice to try to develop a homily on the basis of all three scriptural readings. At best, the attempt requires the accommodated use of the thematic pair or the accommodated reading of the reading from the apostolic writings.[52] At worst, it results in a misunderstanding of a biblical text which is forced into a mold for which it is not suited. While the faithful may be impressed by the homilist's ingenuity, they are really being deprived of the opportunity of having the significance of God's word unfolded for them.

A Long View

When deciding to preach on a reading from Paul's letters or from the apostolic writings, the homilist should take a fairly long view. Good pastoral practice would seem to indicate that it is preferable to preach on a sequence of semi-continuous readings rather than to preach on a single text taken in isolation from the texts read on the previous and following weekends. By preaching from an entire series of semi-continuous readings, the preacher enables the congregation to become familiar with the epistles from which these readings have been taken.

Implementing such a long view is pastorally beneficial. It serves to instruct the faithful about one or another of the New Testament scriptures. The same principle is involved as was involved in the decision to offer the faithful readings from the gospel according to Matthew in Year A, readings from Mark in Year B, and readings from Luke in Year C.

In point of fact, the introduction to the lectionary frequently exhorts the one who presides to take a long view of the scriptures.[53] For example, in those jurisdictions where presiders are allowed, for reasons of pastoral advantage, to choose one lection from either the Old Testament or the apostolic writings, the introduction remarks that "it would hardly be consistent to choose a reading from the Old Testament one week and from the writings of the apostles the next week, with no order or harmony at all."[54]

Similarly, presiders at the weekday eucharist are urged to opt for a text from the semi-continuous reading rather than to make use of another text, even when this alternative text is provided in the lectionary.[55] When a particular celebration interrupts the semi-continuous reading, those who preside at the eucharist during the week are encouraged to consider in advance the entire week's readings so that they might combine passages in such a way as not to deprive the faithful of hearing the word of God in its amplitude.[56]

Taking a long look at the scriptures may require some additional foresight in those communities where a roster of preachers is rotated among the various weekend celebrations of the eucharist. In many communities it is rare that those who gather for the eleven o'clock eucharist on Sunday listen to the same preacher each week. When a community enjoys the availability of more than one homilist, it is important that there be some coordination and cooperation among the various preachers so that, in fact, the eleven o'clock Sunday congregation will have the benefit of listening to a homily based on a letter for the entire series of Sundays during which that particular letter is read.

The Use of a Commentary

Making the decision to preach on a sequence of semi-continuous readings encourages a good preacher to become familiar once again with the biblical texts.[57] Many an instructor of homiletics has suggested that it is good for a homilist, who wishes to be faithful to the scriptures, to take in hand a commentary on the gospel according to Matthew in Year A, a commentary on Mark in Year B, and so forth. Should a homilist decide to allow one of Paul's letters to speak God's word to the people of today, he or she would similarly profit from the use of one or another good commentary on the letters. This kind of long-range preparation for preaching is encouraged by "The Interpretation of the Bible in the Church."

A most effective use of the commentary requires that the homilist read the commentary's general introduction to the letter before beginning a series of homilies based on the semi-continuous sequence of passages from that letter. Becoming familiar with the biblical text in this fashion is a most useful way of preparing to preach.

The use of a commentary in this way is far more important than is consulting the commentary's exegesis of the specific passages to be preached. Reading the general material at the beginning of the commentary allows the homilist to become generally familiar with the letter and to situate it within its real-life situation in Paul's ministry.

In many instances, the use of a good commentary helps to elucidate the points of similarity between Paul's pastoral situation and a pastoral situation. A good homilist is one who is aware of the analogy between the biblical author's situation and that of his or her own congregation. Ernest Best has called this fruitful way of using the scriptures in one's homilies the method of "interpretation parallelism."[58] In fact, the preacher has two worlds in front of him or her, the world of the bible, and the world of the congregation. These two worlds must be brought together in the homily, if the homily is to be both faithful to the word of God and beneficial to the faithful.[59]

The Text That Is Read

Practicality dictates that the homilist be aware of the lectionary text that will, in fact, be read to the congregation. More than one homilist has been surprised when, having carefully prepared a homily, he or she has heard proclaimed a translation of the text that is not the one on which the prepared homily was based.

How well I still remember the vigil service at which my own bishop was present. He was scheduled to preside at an ordination on the following day. The scripture lection chosen for the vigil service was Romans 12:9-18. The New American Bible's translation of that very passage had provided my bishop with his motto, "rejoice in hope" (Rom 12:12). The passage provided me with a theme for my homily. The homily lost much of its verve when the reader dutifully read, from the Jerusalem Bible, "If you have hope, this will make you cheerful." My homiletic refrain had left the church, as it were, in the reader's choice of translation of the scriptural text.

Many homilists have had experiences such as this. This kind of thing happens not only on the occasion of prayer services, where the scriptural texts and translations are chosen ad libitum, but also on the occasion of Sunday eucharist. The Jerusalem Bible, the New American Bible, the Revised Standard Version and the New Revised Standard Version[60] have all been approved for liturgical use.

A visitor to a congregation may not know which translation is in actual use in the congregation to be visited. Even a residential homilist is sometimes surprised by a reader who brings to the lectern his or her own lectionary or version of the Bible. Some readers do this because they prefer to read from a text with which they became familiar as they prepared to exercise their ministry of reader for the benefit of God's people.

Awareness of the translation to be used in the liturgical lection is very important when one is preparing to preach on the semicontinuous reading from the apostolic writings. It is all too easy to read through the epistle from a translation that one has at hand rather than from the translation that will actually be used in the liturgical lections and then to be surprised during the celebration of the liturgy. Moreover, the conscientious homilist who takes the time to prepare a series of homilies based on a semicontinuous reading of the letters may sometimes find it discordant to discover that a carefully scrutinized commentary may relate more readily to one particular translation of a biblical text rather than to another, and that it is this other translation which will actually be read during the celebration of a Sunday morning's eucharistic liturgy.

Letters and Epistles

In my preaching, as in my teaching, I have found it useful to distinguish between "letters" and "epistles." Within the category of letters I would include all of the letters which were actually written by Paul to various churches, that is, his letters to the churches in Thessalonica, Corinth, Galatia, Rome, and Philippi, and to Philemon's house.

Under the rubric of epistles, I would include all of those New Testament texts which have the appearance of letters but are not, in fact, actual correspondence from Paul or one of the other apostolic figures whose names they bear. My category of "epistles" includes "Paul's letters" to Timothy and Titus, as well as the epistles to the Ephesians, the Colossians and the Thessalonians (2 Thessalonians). It would also include the epistle of James, the two epistles of Peter, and the first epistle of John.[61]

The distinction between letters and epistles is a good one for the preacher to bear in mind. The distinction should help the homilist to choose appropriate language, when making reference to these different texts. The lectionary's selection of passages from the apostolic writings for reading in the Sunday liturgical assembly seems to treat the apostolic writings as "epistles," in my understanding of that term. The passages which have been chosen for Sunday reading have something of a timeless character, a quality enhanced by the process of editing them for liturgical use.

Even the passages taken from Paul's genuine letters have been edited for liturgical use in such a way that the person-to-person involvement which characterizes the letters is generally deleted from the lectionary text appointed for Sunday reading. Biographical bits and personal instructions, for example, do not usually appear in the Sunday lectionary. Similarly, Paul's long reflection on food which had been offered to idols (1 Cor 8—10) does not appear in the lectionary. That was a real problem for mid-first century Corinthian Christians, but it is not one of major concern for Christians today.

The Liturgical Order of Readings

If one chooses to preach the gospel on the basis of the apostolic writings, one should be aware that semi-continuous readings appear in the lectionary according to what can be called their liturgical order. The liturgical order of the biblical texts differs both from their canonical order and from their chronological order.

The canonical order of the letters of Paul and the other apostolic writings is well known: Romans, 1 and 2 Corinthians, Galatians, Ephesians, Colossians, Philippians, 1 and 2 Thessalonians, 1 and 2 Timothy, Titus, Philemon, Hebrews, James, 1 and 2 Peter, 1, 2 and 3 John, Jude, Revelation. As far as the letters of Paul are concerned, some scholarly dispute as to the order in which they were written still exists. Nonetheless, one can take as a useful hypothesis the following sequence: 1 Thessalonians, Galatians, 1 Corinthians, 2 Corinthians, Romans, Philemon, Philippians.[62] The Sunday liturgy's semi-continuous reading of Paul's letters and the other apostolic writings follows neither the canonical nor the chronological sequence of the biblical texts.

A variety of pastoral reasons and the liturgical seasons have contributed to the establishment of the liturgical order of readings. In Year A 1 Corinthians, Romans, Philippians, and 1 Thessalonians is the appointed sequence. In Year B it is 1 Corinthians, 2 Corinthians, Ephesians, James, and Hebrews. In Year C the church reads from 1 Corinthians, Galatians, Colossians, Hebrews, Philemon, 1 and 2 Timothy, and 2 Thessalonians. We should note that selections from Paul's first letter to the Corinthians are read in each year of the three-year cycle, and that selections from the epistle to the Hebrews are read in two years (B and C).

Year A

In the first year of the three-year cycle, the very practical first letter to the Corinthians is read at the beginning of the new liturgical year, and continues to be read for seven Sundays (Weeks 2—8). The more visibly eschatologically oriented first letter to the Thessalonians comes at the end of the year. It is read on five successive Sundays (Weeks 29—33). In between comes the reading of Paul's letter to the Romans (Weeks 9—24) and the reading of the letter to the Philippians (Weeks 25—28).

These letters are truly letters. All four of them were written by Paul himself to very real flesh-and-blood congregations. The lectionary text provides the congregation with the opening words of three of these letters, namely, 1 Corinthians, Romans, and 1

Thessalonians. Thus the congregation is made aware that Paul had Sosthenes with him when he wrote to the Corinthians and that he associated Silvanus and Timothy with himself when he wrote to the Thessalonians. Silvanus and Timothy had, of course, been associated with Paul in his evangelization of the community at Thessalonica. In writing to Rome, Paul identifies only himself as one who greets Christians in the capital of the empire.[63]

1 Corinthians

Paul's first letter to the Corinthians is, of all the New Testament texts, the one document which allows us to really get a glimpse of the life and times of a first century Christian community. The letter identifies several members of the community by name. It describes some of the community's activities. It tells about the tensions within the community and the struggles with which it was confronted. Paul learned about the difficulties confronting the community from his visitors, the household of Chloe (1 Cor 1:11) and those who came with Stephanas (1 Cor 16:17). He had also received a letter from the Corinthians (1 Cor 7:1).

Sometime before Paul wrote his "first" letter to the Corinthians, he had written to the Corinthians, urging them not to associate with persons whose sexual mores left something to be desired (1 Cor 5:9).[64] As an expression of his continuing pastoral care for the community, Paul sent Timothy, his closest co-worker, to Corinth (1 Cor 4:17; 16:10). Again he wrote to them, in our "first letter" to the Corinthians. This letter, which Paul clearly considered to be an exercise of his apostolic authority, was written sometime around 54 A.D.

Writing in the Hellenistic manner of his day, Paul summarized what he intended to do in his letter by an appeal to the community to be united in mind and judgment (1 Cor 1:10), the leitmotif of the entire letter and the opening verse of the liturgical reading for the third Sunday of the year. Thereafter Paul took up the various issues which divided the community. At times he appears to be responding to specific questions which the Corinthians themselves had asked.

Among the topics on which Paul reflects and with regard to which he offers a pastoral exhortation are the significance of true wisdom, the role of the apostle, sexual immorality, the use of public courts of law, marriage and virginity, food that has been offered to idols, the celebration of eucharist, charisms and the unity of the community, the idea of Christian love, speaking in tongues, and the reality and importance of the resurrection of Jesus. The first part of this letter (chapters 1–4) is read in Year A. This section of the letter considers the issues of true wisdom and the nature of the apostolate.

Romans

Paul's letter to the Romans stands in sharp contrast with his first letter to the Corinthians. Although it is of approximately the same length as his letter to the Corinthians, it is much more formal than is the letter to the Corinthians. The first letter to the Corinthians deals with many practical issues; the letter to the Romans gives the impression of almost being a theological tract. To a large degree the difference between the two letters is due to the fact that whereas Paul had evangelized the community at Corinth and experienced a continuing pastoral responsibility for those whom he had evangelized, he had never visited the Christian community at Rome. The Roman metropolis had been evangelized by other missionaries.

Paul's letter to the Romans served as an introduction to Paul, prior to his intended visit to the community (Rom 1:9-15; 15:22-24). It is a letter of introduction, but of self-introduction. It is, in fact, a kind of letter-essay in which Paul spells out his vision, especially with regard to what may be called the "Jewish question" in all its complexity. At the time the Christian community at Rome was composed of both Gentile Christians and Jewish Christians. The latter belonged to the relatively large Jewish settlement in Rome, whose members were in frequent contact with Jerusalem. The trade routes and the Augustinian Peace permitted back and forth movement between the capital of the empire and the center of Judaism. Nonetheless, just a few years before

Paul was to write his letter, the emperor Claudius had expelled Jews from Rome because Jews "persisted in rioting at the instigation of Chrestus."[65]

To help him in the actual writing of his long letter, Paul was able to employ the services of a scribe, Tertius (Rom 16:22). The theme of his letter was the good news of the righteousness of God, made manifest in and through Christ. Because it is so comprehensive and so reflective, the letter to the Romans has been called Paul's last will and testament (Günter Bornkamm). Paul begins the letter with an epistolary prescript which may incorporate an ancient credal formula (Rom 1:1-6), a passage designated for liturgical use on the fourth Sunday of Advent (Year A).

In Year A, during a fifteen-week period, beginning with the ninth Sunday in ordinary time, the Sunday eucharistic liturgy features the letter to the Romans. The first passage to be read (Rom 3:21-25, 28; 9th Sunday) is one which exposits the very notion of God's righteousness: Although all people are sinners, they have been justified by God's gift in Christ Jesus. The sole condition for obtaining justification is "faith": a person is justified by faith apart from observance of the law, that is, apart from "works of the law." To make his point, Paul wrote about Jesus' death in terms which evoke redemption wrought by God and the place (the mercy seat) where atonement was made on the feast of Yom Kippur. For Paul, the great example of faith is Abraham (Rom 4:18-25; 10th Sunday). As was the case with Abraham, the promise is fulfilled only for people of faith.

Having announced his theme and illustrated it with the biblical example of Abraham, Paul explains how the love of God assures salvation for those who believe and are justified by faith (Rom 5:1–8:39). Passages from this second major movement in the development of Paul's thought serve as the Sunday scriptures for the eleventh through the eighteenth week of the year. The announcement that, because of the love of God, we have been reconciled through the death of Jesus and are saved through hope of sharing in his life provides the theme for the eleventh Sunday (Rom 5:6-11).

Paul goes on to explain that the new life of the Christian is characterized by freedom from death, sin, and the law, and that it is empowered by the Spirit. The contrast between Adam and Christ shows that new life in Christ brings with it freedom from sin and death (Rom 5:12-15; 12th Sunday). New life in Christ is effected through baptism, which means that death no longer has ultimate power over us and that we are dead to sin (Rom 6:3-4, 8-11; 13th Sunday). The Spirit which empowers this new life is the very Spirit which raised Jesus from the dead. The Spirit frees us from a condition of sinful ("fleshy") existence. Paul does not intend to demean the human body (*sōma*) in which the Spirit dwells. What he does is to set up a sharp contrast between life in the Spirit (*pneuma*) and life in the flesh (*sarx*), that is, life that is prone to sin (Rom 8:9, 11-13; 14th Sunday).

In the magnificent eighth chapter of his letter, Paul expatiates on life in the Spirit. Four passages from this reflection on life in the Spirit serve as the scriptural readings for the fifteenth to the eighteenth Sunday of the year. Paul asserts that three realities attest to our new and future oriented existence: creation in travail, our own hope, and the Spirit itself (Rom 8:18-23; 15th Sunday). In Paul's discussion of the role of the Spirit in the Christian life, he reminds us that the Spirit assists us by assuring that our prayer is properly directed to our God and Father (Rom 8:26-27; 16th Sunday). Since we who are called are conformed to the image of the Son, the firstborn among us, we are destined for glory. That glory is the consummation of the Christian life (Rom 8:28-30; 17th Sunday). Paul brings to closure his long reflection on the justification effected by God in Jesus Christ with a hymn which celebrates the love of God made manifest in Christ Jesus. Excerpts from this hymn provide us with our scripture for the eighteenth Sunday of the year (Rom 8:35, 37-39).

Thereafter Paul turns his attention to Israel, to remind his readers that what God has accomplished in Jesus does not negate his promises to Israel of old (Rom 9:1–11:36). Readings from this section of Paul's letter to the Romans provide the homilist with a good opportunity to reflect on the role of Israel in God's providence. It is an occasion to put to rest anti-semitic prejudice and to correct an erroneous theological supersessionism.[66] Paul laments the situation of his fellow Israelites, yet he cannot help but rehearse a litany of the blessings which are theirs (Rom 9:1-

5; 19th Sunday). If Israel appears to have been rejected, its disbelief is only temporary; in the providence of God his gift and his call are irrevocable (Rom 11:13-15, 29-32; 20th Sunday). Paul concludes his digression on Israel with a hymn which celebrates the mysterious ways of God's providence, a hymn of praise to the wisdom and mercy of God (Rom 11:33-36; 21st Sunday).

Thereafter follows Paul's long exhortation dealing with the moral demands made on those who would live in Christ (Rom 12:1-15:13). The lectionary employs Paul's initial hortatory remark, which reminds us that the truly Christian life is worship of God, almost a kind of liturgy in itself (Rom 12:1-2; 22nd Sunday). According to Paul, it is not only the entire law, but specifically the ten commandments which are summed up in the commandment to love one's neighbor (Rom 12:8-10; 23rd Sunday). One whose life is truly motivated by love fulfills the requirements of the law. To live the Christian life is to acknowledge Jesus as Lord. Ultimately the one who lives as the servant of Jesus the Lord will share in the glory of the Lord himself (Rom 14:7-9; 24th Sunday).

Philippians

Paul's letter to the Philippians provides the church with scriptural readings for the twenty-fifth to the twenty-ninth Sundays of the year. Scholars debate as to whether Paul wrote his letter from Ephesus in about 56 A.D. or whether it was written from Rome in the early 60s. Similarly they dispute among themselves as to whether the letter was a single composition by Paul or whether the letter in its canonical form is a composite of various (three) letter fragments written by Paul. Fortunately, the resolution of these moot issues does not significantly affect the interpretation of the passages chosen by the church for its Sunday liturgy.

Paul was, in any case, in prison when he wrote to the Philippians. The pangs of someone facing death are reflected in the liturgy's first reading from the letter (Phil 1:20-24, 27; 25th Sunday). Paul's relationship with the church at Philippi was a particularly close one. Those bonds are reflected in the reading for the twenty-sixth Sunday (Phil 2:1-11). The reading culminates in the magnificent Christological hymn, which also serves the church's liturgy on Passion Sunday. In his letter Paul reminds the Christians at Philippi that prayer and the virtuous life are the hallmarks of Christian existence, as his own life has attested (Phil 4:6-9; 27th Sunday). As he brings his letter to a close, Paul again draws attention to his suffering and the support which he has received from the Philippians. This elicits a prayer, one of petition and of praise (Phil 4:12-14, 19-20; 28th Sunday).

1 Thessalonians

The readings for Year A conclude with a selection from the first of Paul's letters, the oldest piece of Christian literature, his letter to the Thessalonians (50 A. D.) The first part of the letter (1 Thess 1–3; 29th-31st Sundays) rehearses Paul's warm memories of his visit to Thessalonica. It recalls the faithful and enthusiastic response made by the Thessalonians to Paul's preaching of the gospel.

As would become customary for him to do, Paul devoted the second part of his letter to a series of moral exhortations. Two of these address a matter that was particularly problematic for the new Christians at Thessalonica. What were they to expect once some of their number had begun to die, perhaps as a result of some local hostility? Paul responds that the fate of the dead is in the hands of God. The Christian need not fear since God will raise from the dead those who have died in Christ, just as Jesus had been raised from the dead (1 Thess 4:13-18; 32nd Sunday). In the meantime Christians are to get on with their lives, living as children of the light. The day of the Lord will surely come—like a thief in the night!—but Christians are to live as the children of the day, for that is their calling (1 Thess 5:1-6; 33rd Sunday).

5

What About Next Year?
Preaching Years B & C

In Year B, when the gospel according to Mark is read, the lectionary's sequence of New Testament readings begins with 1 Corinthians, as it did in Year A. The liturgy's reading from the letter continues from the place where it had been broken off in Year A (1 Cor 5). Following the five readings from this first letter to the Corinthians (Weeks 2-6) comes a series of readings from Paul's second letter to the Corinthians (Weeks 7-14). Concentration on the situation of the church at Corinth from the perspective of both 1 Corinthians and that of 2 Corinthians enables modern-day listeners to better appreciate the back-and-forth, up-and-down, give-and-take nature of the relationship that existed between the apostle and the community of Christians in the Achaian metropolis.

More on 1 Corinthians

Although the readings from 1 Corinthians appointed for the Sunday celebrations in Year B may pose a particular problem for those who worship at St. Augustin's in Des Moines, they do provide the homilist with a unique opportunity for reflecting on some of the implications of our faith. Three of the readings are taken from the section of Paul's letter in which he speaks about human sexuality (1 Cor 5–7). The first of these (1 Cor 6:13-15, 17-20) draws our attention to the dignity of the human body, the temple of the Spirit. Our bodies, with their sexual aspects, belong to the Lord. It is as human beings with gender and sexuality that we belong to the body of Christ. The second reading (1 Cor 7:29-

31) invites us to consider all human realities, our sexual relationships, our emotions, our economic condition, indeed everything that is human, in the light of the eschaton. Marriage, sadness, buying and selling are part of life, but they are not ultimate reality, no matter how this world tries to make sexual satisfaction, emotional well-being, or economic ability the absolute norm of human existence.

The third reading (1 Cor 7:32-35) extols virginity. The congregation at St. Augustin's should not come away from the celebration of the liturgy with the idea that marriage is of lesser value than celibacy in the eyes of God, but they should realize that there is tremendous value in the unmarried state, whether this be in the form of consecrated celibacy within the church, the unmarried state for the sake of service to others in the pursuit of one's own career, or a reasoned assessment of one's own sexuality. No one should feel pressured to marry because that is the thing to do. Rather all must devote themselves entirely to the Lord.

The next two readings are taken from Paul's reflection on the nature of his own ministry (1 Cor 9:16-19, 22-23; 10:31–11:1). Paul offers himself as an example to be imitated. Would that all Christians, and all preachers, could do the same! Paul's words about preaching the gospel provides the homilist with an occasion to preach about full-time ministry within the church, about the church's need for missionaries and religious. These are special "vocations"; yet the homilist should always remain aware that each and every Christian has a proper vocation in the Lord. Whatever we do, we must do all for the glory of God.

And Something on 2 Corinthians

An ever increasing number of scholars are convinced that the present format of Paul's second letter to the Corinthians is the result of an unknown editor's compilation of several significant portions of Paul's ongoing correspondence with the Christians of Corinth.[67] According to this kind of analysis, much of the extant second letter to the Corinthians was derived from an apology, that is, a reasoned defense of himself and his teaching, which Paul directs to the Corinthians in 2 Cor 2:14–6:13 and 7:2-4.

This apology provides the church with scriptural readings on the seventh through the fourteenth Sundays of Year B. As an apostle, Paul describes himself as a minister of the new covenant. For Paul, the very existence of the Christian community at Corinth was living proof that the Spirit of the living God was active in his ministry (2 Cor 3:1-6), whose purpose was to make known the glory of God. Well aware that God chose the weak in the world to shame the strong (1 Cor 1:27), Paul is not disinclined to speak of his human weakness in order to witness thereby to the power of God (2 Cor 4:6-11). With faith in God, Paul has preached for the benefit of the Corinthians. He proclaims that God who raised Jesus from the dead will likewise raise the Corinthian Christians, along with Paul, so that all might dwell together in the heavenly sanctuary (2 Cor 4:13–5:11). Paul's faith was the source of his unbounded confidence; his sole aim in life was to please the Lord (2 Cor 5:6-10). It was the love of Christ, manifest in his death for the benefit of all, that moved Paul to preach and act as he did. Christ's resurrection, which ushers in the new creation, provides a new and different perspective on all that exists (2 Cor 5:14-17).

According to the compilation-theory of understanding 2 Corinthians, a second apology, to which Paul's mention of a "tearful letter" in 2 Corinthians 2:4 may well refer, is represented in 2 Corinthians 10:1-13:10. This apology provides us with a scriptural reading for the fourteenth Sunday of the year. As he did in 1 Corinthians and in his letter to the Philippians, Paul once again proclaims that because he is powerless, the power of Christ rests upon him. Enigmatic references to the thorn in the flesh and the angel of Satan point to the difficulties encountered by Paul in the exercise of his ministry, a ministry beset not only by his own weakness, but also by mistreatment, distress, persecution, and a variety of other difficulties.

That Paul found it necessary to write to the Corinthians in his own defense is an indication that all was not always well between himself and some members of the Christian community in the Achaian metropolis. At one point Paul appears to have sent them a letter of reconciliation, which provides the canonical second letter to the Corinthians with its epistolary framework (2 Cor 1:1–2:13; 7:5-16; 13:11-13). From this letter of reconciliation the church takes its scriptural reading for the seventh Sunday of the year (2 Cor 1:18-22).[68] In this passage Paul proclaims that the gospel proclaimed by him and his companions, Silvanus and Timothy, is unambiguous. God's fidelity to his people is fulfilled in Christ. In our common prayer, for which we are enabled by the Spirit given in baptism, we say yes to God. This is our Amen. With its subtle allusions to the church's common prayer and to the baptism in the Spirit which conforms us to Christ, the reading for the seventh Sunday of the year gives an occasion for the homilist to speak about the role of liturgy and sacrament as a response to the preaching of the gospel.

Two so-called administrative letters provide the text for the eighth and ninth chapters of Paul's second letter to the Corinthians. These chapters deal with the collection for the church in Jerusalem, a perennial concern of the apostle Paul. The reading for the thirteenth Sunday of the year (2 Cor 8:7, 9, 13-15) describes the challenge of Christian charity with marvelous theological clarity and in terms which express the practicality of common-sense wisdom.

After the selection of readings from Paul's Corinthian correspondence comes the semicontinuous reading of three texts that were not written by the apostle, namely, Ephesians (Weeks 15-21), James (Weeks 22-26), and Hebrews (Weeks 27-33). The reading of these New Testament books provides the Christian congregation with an opportunity to become familiar with three apostolic writings, whose character is among the least letter-like among the New Testament "epistles." These texts, a theological treatise (Ephesians), an extended moral exhortation (James), and a homily (Hebrews), are also among the New Testament texts which, historically speaking, are the furthest removed from the apostolic figure to which tradition has linked them.

Year C

With its readings from eight different epistles, Year C provides the homilist with a potpourri of Pauline texts. As it did in each of the two previous liturgical years, the lectionary sequence begins with a continuation of the semi-continuous reading of Paul's first letter to the Corinthians, picking up at the juncture which had been interrupted in Year B (1 Corinthians 10). By continuing its reading from 1 Corinthians for another seven weeks (Year C, Weeks 2-8), the liturgy gives further expression to Paul's pastoral response to a very human community that was caught up in a variety of problems and concerns.

Still More from 1 Corinthians

The readings from Paul's first letter to the Corinthians on the first seven Sundays of the year are taken from two discrete sections of his correspondence, namely, chapters 12–14, where Paul writes about the unity and diversity of the church, making use of the graphic analogy of the human body to remind his readers that there is a vital unity which requires and makes use of the diversity of its members, and chapter 15, where Paul deals at length with the significance of the resurrection of Jesus.

In his rehearsal of the various gifts given to the members of the church at Corinth, Paul highlights their source and purpose. The several gifts are given to individual members of the community—and no member of the community is without a gift!—but they spring from a common source, namely, the Spirit of God. These gifts are given to various members of the community, but they are given for the common good, for building up the body of Christ, as the author of the epistle to the Ephesians would say (Eph 4:12). Paul's reflections in this regard provide a variety of homiletic opportunities for one who preaches at St. Augustine's in Pleasanton. He or she may want to remind the congregation that every baptized Christian is, in a radical sense, a charismatic Christian. Alternatively, this may be a good occasion to reflect on the kind of authentic Christian community which each parish ought to be, using the gifts and talents of its several members for the benefit of all. Then again, Paul's words may prompt the homilist to look at the wider church and reflect on the charisms of the several religious congregations which are so vital to the life and mission of the church today.

The Week of Prayer for Christian Unity occurs at about the same time that the church is reading from those sections of Paul's letter which deal with the unity and diversity of the church. Identifying the several gifts of the various Christian communities might be a profitable pastoral exercise at this time of the year. On the other hand, Paul's words about the body of Christ remind all Christians of our need for one another. His own reflections point to baptism as the sacramental source of our unity. His enumeration of several charisms lists the apostles first, an emphasis that reminds us of the apostolic heritage and mission of the entire body of Christ.

The most basic of all the charisms is love, extolled by Paul in the paean of love found in 1 Corinthians 13. The passage is often read and preached during nuptial celebrations, but it has an ecclesial importance. The church is a community of love; in all that it does it is called to be the instrument of God, allowing his love to be active and present in the world. In this respect, Paul offers himself as an example of how God's love is at work in the church.

1 Corinthians 15 furnishes four readings (Weeks 5 to 8) which highlight the centrality of the resurrection of Jesus as the object of Christian faith. Vatican Council II vigorously proclaimed the importance of the resurrection, and reminded us that each Sunday's eucharistic celebration is, in fact, a celebration of the paschal mystery. Yet it is all too easy to preach about the resurrection of Jesus only on Easter Sunday and then, perhaps, to concentrate almost exclusively on the discovery of the empty tomb. Weeks 5 to 8 of Year C allow us an opportunity to bring matters into sharper focus.

The reading of 1 Corinthians 15:1-11 serves as a strong reminder that the gospel, the good news of our salvation, has the death and resurrection of Jesus as its focal point. Recalling the credal formula which Paul had passed along to the Corinthians reminds us of the centrality of the common creed in the life of the church. On the other hand, Paul's words remind us that the resurrection of Jesus is not so much the end of a story as it is the beginning of a story, the story of the church and of our salvation.

The Nicean creed proclaims our common faith in the resurrection of the body, a truth poorly understood by so many of the faithful. Paul teaches that the resurrection of Jesus is the ground of the resurrection of those who have died in Christ and the source of our hope (1 Cor 15:12, 16-20). To show the ultimate centrality of Christ, Paul often has recourse to Adam, with whom Christ can be compared and contrasted. The risen Christ is the one who gives life; the risen Christ is the one with whom we are to be conformed (1 Cor 15:45-49). Death, like taxes, is inevitable. It is a reality about which we humans find it difficult to speak. It is, nonetheless, one of those realities of life about which Paul writes in his letter to the Corinthians. He invites us to consider death in the light of the resurrection of Jesus and our own resurrection.

Galatians

After 1 Corinthians, the lectionary sequence in Year C provides semi-continuous readings from Galatians (Weeks 9-14), Colossians (Weeks 15-18), Hebrews (Weeks 19-22), Philemon (Week 23), 1 Timothy (Weeks 24-26), 2 Timothy (Weeks 27-30), and 2 Thessalonians (Weeks 31-33).

Paul's letter to the Galatians is one of the oldest Christian texts to deal with the issue of religious freedom and to explain the nature of real liberty. This letter may well be the most passionate of all Paul's letters. In it Paul is alternatively threatened, defensive, angry, aggressive, and challenging. The strong feelings which Paul expresses make of the letter to the Galatians a vivid witness to the kind of person and apostle that Paul really was.

The opening of the letter already shows the vehemence of Paul's emotions (Gal 1:1-10). In it he defends his apostolate and proclaims that there is but a single gospel (9th Sunday). In the body of his letter Paul discusses the truth of the gospel (Gal 1:11–2:21), focusing first upon his own apostolic call and ministry, then on justification by faith. These topics are rehearsed on the tenth and eleventh Sundays of the year. We are justified by faith. Whose faith? According to the classic interpretation of Galatians 2:16 we are justified as a result of our faith in Jesus Christ. The classic interpretation of Paul's words continues to be maintained by a number of scholars, but many scholars—most notably a growing number of American exegetes—interpret Galatians 2:16 to mean that we are justified because of the fidelity of Jesus Christ.[69]

In the second major section of the letter to the Galatians, Galatians 3:1–5:12, Paul deals with the children of the promise. His exposition is represented in our lectionary by a passage in which Paul explains that those who are baptized are children of God and descendants of Abraham and Sarah (Gal 3:26-29; 12th Sunday). Again there is a problem in understanding the phrase which the New American Bible has translated "faith in Christ Jesus" (Gal 3:26). Recent translations, including the revision of the NAB, take the expression, "in Christ Jesus," as a phrase which modifies the entire sentence rather than as a phrase which qualifies our faith. It is in Christ Jesus that we are children of God—a very important theological affirmation indeed!

The third major section of the letter to the Galatians deals with life in the Spirit and Christian love (Gal 5:13–6:10). We are free to love, says Paul, and that is the theme of the scriptural reading for the thirteenth Sunday of the Year (Gal 5:1, 13-18). Paul brings the letter to the Galatians to closure with a handwritten note, added to the text which the scribe had written from Paul's dictation (Gal 6:11-18). The note includes a brief reflection on the new creation and Paul's farewell greetings, the topic of the scriptural reading for the fourteenth Sunday of the year.

The year's final medley of texts (Weeks 24-33: 1 Tim, 2 Tim, 2 Thess) begins with a passage from 1 Timothy 1:12-17 that presents a stylized picture of Paul, the great sinner who had become a great saint.[70] The author's portrayal of Paul presents the homilist with another occasion when our tradition's reception of Paul might be the subject of homiletic exposition. If so, the occasion might well be one in which the homilist would briefly touch upon the phenomenon of Pauline pseudepigraphy. The occasion would be particularly propitious insofar as the reading from 1

Timothy 1 on the twenty-fourth Sunday of the year introduces a sequence of ten readings from the Pauline pseudepigrapha.

The sequence includes three passages of the second epistle to the Thessalonians (Weeks 31-33). The eschatological focus of this epistle brings Year C's sequence of readings to proper liturgical closure. It also provides an appropriate eschatological and forward-looking note for the entire three-year cycle of New Testament readings before it celebrates the Feast of Christ the King with the pantocratic vision of the exalted Christ provided by the author of the anonymous letter to the Colossians.

6

What To Do
on Festive Occasions

With the exception of the five Sundays in Year B, when we listen to a reading from the epistle of James, the semi-continuous sequence appointed as the series of second readings for Sundays in ordinary time is taken from the Pauline corpus. In Easter time the lectionary offers a series of semi-continuous readings from the first letter of Peter (Year A), the first letter of John (Year B), and the book of Revelation (Year C).

In each year of the liturgical cycle, the Sunday liturgy's New Testament readings for Easter time are taken from post-apostolic texts with which tradition has associated the name of one of the apostles.[71] The first epistle of Peter begins with the identification of Peter, its patronym, as "an apostle of Jesus Christ" (1 Pet 1:1). The epistolary opening of this text, including its identification of the putative sender and recipients, along with greetings for the latter (1 Pet 1:1-2), is not, however, used in the Sunday lectionary.

The first epistle of John begins with a preface (1 John 1:1-4), akin to the preface of the fourth gospel (John 1:1-18), but this preface does not appear in the lectionary. In any case, the first epistle of John does not make any claim whatsoever to have been written by a man named John, let alone by John, the son of Zebedee.

Another text from the Johannine corpus, the book of Revelation, serves as reading material for the Easter season in Year C. The lectionary has once again not appropriated the opening of this book (Rev 1:1-3); its reading from the book of Revelation begins with the presentation of "John,"[72] a preacher and witness to Jesus, in exile on the island of Patmos, who is an extraordinary seer indeed (Rev 1:9-11, 12-13, 17-19). The preacher who is concerned for the well-being of the congregation might be encouraged to seize this occasion, the second Sunday of Easter (Year C), to talk about the function of apocalyptic language and literature in the life of the church. At the very least he or she might want to spell out for the people the important distinction between "Revelation" and "revelations." So many people call the last book in the New Testament the book of Revelations, as if the seer of Patmos had been the beneficiary of several distinct revelations, knowledge of which must now be shared with the Christian congregations of our day. The book of Revelation is not a collection of revelations; it is an apocalypse, an expression of faith and hope for a beleaguered community living in uncertain times.

What has been said about the semi-continuous readings from the Pauline texts is analogously applicable to each of the series of readings from the apostolic writings appointed for the Easter season. In each year of the cycle selections from a single apostolic writing are heard by the congregation on six successive Sundays. Thus it behooves the homilist to choose to preach from these writings on the entire succession of Sundays and to prepare for the Sunday homilies with the help of a good commentary.

Year A: 1 Peter

The lectionary's selection of readings from the first epistle of Peter is particularly appropriate for the Easter season. Parts of the first epistle of Peter appear to have the characteristics of baptismal homilies. Some authors consider the epistle to be a pastiche of various baptismal homilies that have been incorporated into a single text in the form of a letter,[73] under the authority of the legendary Peter, the patronym for the collection. The baptismal atmosphere which pervades the reading of this epistle makes it singularly appropriate for the Easter season, just after the solemn baptism of the catechumens during the Easter vigil service, at a time when all Christians recall their baptisms. Readings from the first epistle of Peter are especially fitting in the

Easter season of Year A, when the liturgical lections are most suitable for a parish community's celebration of the Rite of Christian Initiation of Adults (RCIA).

On the practical side, a wise homilist should be aware that in the lectionary's sequence of semi-continuous readings from the first letter of Peter, the reading from 1 Peter 2:20-25 on the fourth Sunday of Easter precedes the reading of 1 Peter 2:4-9, which occurs on the fifth Sunday. Something similar happens on the second Sunday of the Easter season in Year B, when a reading from the end of the first epistle of John appears at the beginning of the semi-continuous reading of the text.[74]

The name of Peter appears only in this opening verse of the letter, but the opening of the letter does not appear in the "lectionary text" of 1 Peter. As a matter of fact, the epistle's powerful exhortation on the pastoral ministry, with its description of the author as a fellow elder who is a witness of the sufferings of Christ and who now shares in eschatological glory (1 Pet 5:1-5), has not made its way into the Sunday lectionary either.

Year B: 1 John

In Year B, the reading from 1 John 5:1-6 comes before the other readings that are taken from that epistle for the Sundays of Easter time. Appointed for the second Sunday of Easter, it sets the tone for the weeks to come. When a homilist looks carefully at the lectionary's selection of the six readings from 1 John, he or she will quickly become aware of just how important taking a long view of the scriptures is important for the homilist who wants to preach well.

Not a few preachers of my acquaintance have been caught short during the summer Sundays of Year B, when they first discovered that the Johannine narrative of the multiplication of loaves (John 6:1-15) is followed by a series of five successive excerpts from the discourse on the bread of life. Many of these homilists have given their "eucharistic homily" either on the occasion of the reading of the multiplication story or after the reading of the first excerpt from the bread of life discourse.

Coming up short with fresh ideas for the following Sunday has taught a lesson that is not easily forgotten. Veteran homilists readily recall that the Johannine feeding narrative in Year B is but the beginning of a sequence of tightly interwoven readings on the Johannine theme of the bread of life.

The fourth gospel has a tendency to rehearse many of the same themes over and over again. Some authors therefore speak of the cyclical character of the evangelist's exposition. The tendency to replay variations on a same theme is also characteristic of the first letter of John. The lectionary's selection of seemingly repetitive readings for the Sundays in Easter time reflects the tendency of the biblical text itself.

The reading from 1 John 5:1-6, strategically assigned to the second Sunday of Easter, introduces a number of baptismal themes, not the least of which are 1) the status of Christians as children of God and 2) life characterized by love as the expression of authentic Christian existence. These motifs are then played out in the readings which follow on the next few Sundays. As the themes of God's love for us and our keeping the commandments are unfolded in the various exhortations for Christians to love one another on the last three Sundays of Easter time (see 1 John 3:18-24; 4:7-10; 4:11-16), an inexperienced homilist might find the readings repetitive and shy away from basing a homily upon them.

On the other hand, an experienced homilist might choose to seize the opportunity which these readings present. They afford the homilist a wonderful chance to reflect on the relationship between love and the commandments, on love for one another as a response to God's love for us, on love within the community and love for those outside the community, on love and moral demand, on the various expressions of love which characterize truly Christian relationships, and so forth.

These readings allow the homilist to preach on Christian morality—or, more appropriately phrased, "the Christian way of life"—in the depth and breadth of it. In matters of morality there are relatively few opportunities for preachers to get to the heart of moral discourse, but the Sundays of Easter time in Year B are ready made for the occasion.

How well I remember the directives with regard to sermons that were in force in my home diocese prior to the liturgical renewal inspired by Vatican Council II. One year the sermons were to be preached on the creed, the following year on morality, and the third year on the sacraments. A booklet of suggested sermon outlines was provided for each year in the three year cycle. Because of their perceived need to explain things to the people, many of my contemporaries in the priesthood pine with nostalgia for the old system. Many of them think that, because pastors are expected to preach "a homily," the congregation has been deprived of the instruction which it needs. To be sure a homily is of a different genre from a lesson in moral theology, but many of the foundational elements of basic Christian morality can readily be exposed to any congregation by a pastor who chooses to preach on the Johannine readings during the Easter season.

Revelation

Another great pastoral opportunity is afforded by the Easter readings of Year C. In his Warren lecture at the University of Tulsa, Richard McBrien, then chair of the department of theology of Notre Dame University, remarked that biblical fundamentalism may be the single most serious threat to the Catholic faith in the United States today. Hundreds of thousands of Catholics have been lost to the Catholic Church because of biblical fundamentalism.[75]

The book of Revelation is one of the most popular books in the hands of fundamentalists. For them it is a most useful tool. When the book of Revelation is read in a naively literalistic manner and presumed to offer "revelations" for our times, it poses a real threat to the faith of many a Catholic, particularly among the large Hispanic and Latino Catholic populations in the United States.

Unfortunately most members of Catholic congregations in the United States are almost totally ignorant of what might be called a Catholic reading of the book of Revelation. Until rather recently a Catholic reading of Revelation has been rather difficult to come by. Relatively simple, really good, and up-to-date English language commentaries on Revelation have not been available.[76] This lack made it difficult for most people to read the book of Revelation from a form critical point of view, as it must be read if it is to be understood properly. All too many pastors and religious education directors were also unfamiliar with the book of Revelation. As a result, the Catholic population at large generally lacked the resources to understand this book, which is so intriguing and so threatening.

Among Catholics there exists, nonetheless, a thirst for a much greater knowledge of the book of Revelation. When I visit various parish communities, I am often invited to join in the ongoing bible study group. Almost inevitably, with myself as an "expert" present, questions arise with regard to this book. Prompted by their discussions with friends and neighbors, and intrigued by the media evangelists, they want to know more about what has been rightly called the most enigmatic book in the Bible.

The Sundays of Easter in Year C provide a golden opportunity to address this pastoral need. The Easter Sundays of Year C are prime time, available to the church leader to reflect, in systematic fashion, with the congregation on the book of Revelation. Apart from the Sundays of the Easter season in Year C, the book of Revelation does not often appear in the church's lectionary.[77] In the Sunday and feast day lectionary, a reading from the book of Revelation (Rev 1:5-8) is assigned for the feast of Christ the King (Year B), while the reading of Revelation 7:2-4, 9-14 is appointed as the first reading on the feast of All Saints.

Although the avowed purpose of my present work is to reflect on the preaching of those New Testament texts traditionally called "epistles," the obvious pastoral need and the opportunity provided by the Easter Sundays of Year C prompt me to write a few words about preaching the book of Revelation.

In Year C, the first three readings from the book of Revelation provide a great opportunity for a homilist to reflect on the nature of apocalyptic literature.[78] These readings speak about visions and an enigmatic scroll. Symbols and symbolic numbers abound. On the second and third Sundays, the readings begin, "I, John" (Rev 1:9; 5:11). The first of these readings (Rev 1:9-11, 12-13, 17-

19) especially lends itself to a homilist's explanation of the nature of apocalyptic literature and, specifically, to an explanation of the nature and function of the book of Revelation.

Given the present pastoral situation, one could suggest that leaders of the church have a serious pastoral responsibility to take advantage of the readings from the book of Revelation to speak with the congregation about the nature of apocalyptic literature and how apocalyptic literature functions in the church's life and tradition.

Church leaders become anxious when members of their communities abandon their pursuit of a full and authentic Christian life because they either do not agree with the church's teaching on divorce or abortion or because they do not abide by this teaching in the conduct of their own lives. As a result, many preachers believe themselves duty-bound to address the issues of divorce and abortion from the pulpit, even at the expense of the Sunday homily. In point of fact, Catholic Christians throughout the world are leaving the church in droves. To a large extent the exodus is due to their inability to integrate the book of Revelation into their lives in a truly (Catholic) faith-filled manner. Alas, all too often, and for many leaders of the church, this situation appears not to provoke any great amount of pastoral concern.

The church's liturgy, nonetheless, invites us to reflect on the book of Revelation on the Sundays of the Easter season (Year C). The readings on the first three Sundays project a very rich Christology, albeit one that is expressed in symbolic language. The last three readings from Revelation are taken from the twenty-first chapter of the book. In symbolic language, they speak of Christian hope. Such an expression of Christian hope is a function of the Christian apocalypse. Is there not a need for the Christian message of hope in a world which is as filled with hopelessness and despair as is ours? Is there, in other words, not a real pastoral need for an "Apocalypse Now"?

One who preaches on hope on the basis of the biblical texts which use symbolic language to express the inexpressible should remember the words of visionaries such as trito-Isaiah and Paul the apostle who wrote, "Eye has not seen, ear has not heard, nor has it so much as dawned on man what God has prepared for those who love him" (1 Cor 2:9, NAB),[79] a scripture that is read to the congregation which assembles on the sixth Sunday of the year (Year A). We can tell it like it is, but we cannot tell it as it shall be.

Preaching on Feast Days from Isolated Texts

When the church celebrates its feasts and some of its festal seasons the selection of scriptural readings appointed for the liturgy is often made on the basis of their putative thematic harmony with the feast of the day or the festal season. The selection has been made so as to provide a focus for homiletic reflection.[80]

It is especially during the Advent and Christmas[81] seasons, as well as during Lent and the sacred triduum, that the choice of readings from the apostolic writings has been primarily made on the basis of their thematic harmony with the feast or season to be celebrated. On some occasions, Palm Sunday, the sacred triduum, and during the Christmas season, the same selection of readings from the apostolic writings is appointed to be read in all three years of the liturgical cycle. On the four Sundays of Advent and on the first four Sundays of Lent, however, a different reading from the writings is assigned for each year of the cycle.

Rather than rehearsing the fact that the readings have been appointed on the basis of their thematic harmony with the feast of the day, I would like to identify them as "discontinuous readings." The selection process, for appropriate pastoral reasons, has totally removed the chosen passage from its biblical context. What the lectionary offers is a discontinuous anthology of biblical texts.

Since the second reading of the feast or season is taken from the apostolic writings, the passages are treated—in terms of the distinction made in the previous chapter—as if they were excerpts from epistles rather than as excerpts from letters. Taken out of context by the lectionary, these readings seem to enunciate a timeless message, rather than the real-life response of a pastor in dialogue with a flesh and blood congregation.

When readings from the apostolic writings are chosen on the

basis of the principle of thematic harmony, they function as variants on a theme. Frequently they do not so much coalesce with the first and third readings of the day, as do they attempt to provide a different angle of vision on the feast that is being celebrated. They offer different insights into its major themes.

The Feast of the Epiphany (Eph 3:2-3, 5-6)

On the feast of the Epiphany, for example, the reading of Ephesians 3:2-3, 5-6 is mandated for each of the three years of the liturgical cycle. The text's affirmation that "the Gentiles are now coheirs with the Jews, members of the same body, and sharers of the promise through the preaching of the gospel" (Eph 3:6), coheres with the trito-Isaian vision of men and women of the nations, along with their kings, streaming to Jerusalem in all its glory (Isa 60:1-6). It is likewise consistent with the Matthean tale of magi coming from the east in order to pay homage to the newborn king of the Jews (Matt 2:1-12).

Taken together, the three readings present a marvelous panorama of the universality of salvation. The graphic images of Isaiah and of Matthew vividly portray the reality which is stated so simply by the author of the epistle to the Ephesians. In Christ Jesus we are all one body. The idea is so startling that the author of Ephesians has apparently coined a new word in order to convey the idea. The neologism is *sussōma*, literally, "co-body," rendered in the New American Bible as "members of the same body."

Can one think of a better idea for the first Sunday of a new year than the idea that members of all races are one in Christ Jesus? It is this idea that the church places before us by offering a reading from the epistle to the Ephesians on the feast of the Epiphany.[82]

Out of Step with the Feast

Were one's Epiphany homily to focus principally on the revelation of the mystery per se (Eph 3:4), the homilist would be departing from the theme which the liturgy suggests as the principal theme of the day. Since the lections for feast days such as the Epiphany have been chosen on the basis of their thematic harmony with a specific liturgical celebration, a certain amount of discordance would be present were a homilist to preach on a theme other than that which arises from the readings themselves.

It is wise for the homilist to recall that the days on which the Sunday lectionary chooses readings on the basis of their thematic unity are precisely the days when the Christian church is celebrating or preparing to celebrate the mystery of our salvation in as intense a manner as seems to be liturgically possible. As the church lives its moments of radical self-consciousness and ultimate self-expression it is really inappropriate for a homilist to turn to another subject. How well I remember that particular Sunday when I was invited to relieve some of the pastor's burden by celebrating three of the six weekend masses in the parish. The pastor advised me that there would be no need for me to preach. In place of the sermon on that particular Sunday, various members of the parish finance committee were to address the parish's need for money. As a visitor, I had nothing to say. Since then, however, I have often thought, "Was parish finances the most appropriate theme for a sermon on the feast of Pentecost?"

7

Letters and Life

I once heard a famous preacher remark that most sermons deal with morality, and that thereafter the most frequent concern of the typical Sunday homily is the church. Less frequently do people hear a homily about Christ or about God. After making this reflection, the preacher paused for a moment and then added, "But the proportion should be just the inverse."

There is more than a small measure of truth in what this preacher had to say. All too often preachers adopt a moralizing stance. When they do so, their pastoral option clearly projects the opinion that Christianity is essentially concerned with morality. The reverse side of this coin is that Christian faith seems to have little to do with grace and salvation.[83] We have nonetheless been reminded that "Preaching will perform a task more useful and more conformed to the bible if it helps the faithful above all to know the gift of God' (John 4:10) as it has been revealed in Scripture."[84] The biblical message should preserve its principal characteristic of being the good news of salvation freely offered by God.[85] From this flows the human responsibility to live a truly Christian moral life.

Faith Working Through Love

I do not mean to imply that Christian faith has nothing to do with how we interact with one another. It certainly does. How we relate to one another is a consequence and reflection of how we relate to God. Paul went right to the heart of the matter when, writing to the Galatians, he said, "in Christ Jesus, neither circumcision nor uncircumcision counts for anything, but only faith working through love" (Gal 5:6).

In the earliest of his letters, the first to the Thessalonians, written fairly soon after he had evangelized that Macedonian community, Paul reminisced about his visit to them. He recalled how he had proclaimed the gospel to them. Then he reflected on the fact that he and his companions had, in paternal fashion,[86] urged the Thessalonians to lead a life worthy of the God who was calling them into his kingdom and glory (1 Thess 2:9-12). Later on in that same letter, Paul reminded the Thessalonians that he had challenged them to live in a way that would please God. Father and pastor that he was, he reminded the Thessalonians that he had previously given them instructions as to how they should live. Paul's reminder (1 Thess 4:1-2) is read to the people in the pews on the first Sunday of Advent (Year C).

Paul's reflections stem from his Jewish heritage. To be a Jew is to live like a Jew. It is to live in covenant with God and in relationship with other members of the covenanted people. The covenant (berith) brings horizontal and vertical relationships together in interpenetrating fashion. As a covenantal formula, the ten commandments (Exod 20:1-17; Deut 5:6-21) clearly express the mutually interdependent dual relationship. The first commandments deal with one's relationship with God, the latter commandments with one's relationship with the neighbor. You can't have the one without the other.

According to the triple tradition of the gospels, Jesus reiterated the interdependence of these two basic relationships. When asked about the most important of the commandments, Jesus replied: "This is the first: 'Hear, O Israel! The Lord our God is Lord alone! Therefore you shall love the Lord your God with all your heart, with all your soul, with all your mind, and with all your strength.' This is the second: 'You shall love your neighbor as yourself'" (Mark 12:28-35).[87] Jesus was asked about a single commandment. His response was that there is not one single commandment; there are two and the two go together.

Life in the Real World

What does it mean to live so as to please God in the post-apostolic age? What does it mean to lead a life worthy of God at a time when the Christian community no longer expects the parousia at any moment in the immediate future? What does it mean to live as a disciple of Jesus when one no longer lives in the Jewish culture of first century Palestine? How does one get on with one's life in a Christian fashion when one must live in the "real world"?

These are our questions. They were also the questions of the second and third generation of Christians. It was to answer questions such as these that many of the deutero-Pauline epistles (Ephesians, Colossians, 2 Thessalonians, 1 and 2 Timothy, and Titus) were written. To be sure, this was not the sole purpose for which these epistles were written, but it was one of the main reasons which led to their being written. They were written for people for whom the zeal of their conversion was a personal memory from their past, people for whom the proclamation of the imminent coming of God's reign was but a memory preserved by Christian tradition.

Some scholars write about the bourgeois quality of the moral discourse contained in the deutero-Pauline literature. The way of life of which these epistles speak seems to project an ideal of good citizenship and common sense wisdom, rather than the dynamism of the call to conversion.

Scholars who write in this fashion are sometimes motivated by a concern to show that these epistles were not written by the apostle himself. Others who do so hope to show that these deutero-Pauline epistles are less important than the letters which the apostle himself had written. This is not the place to pursue the scholarly discussion, nor is it the place to take issue with the narrowness of these approaches. This is, however, the place to recall that these deutero-Pauline texts are part of the canon of New Testament scriptures, that they are inspired by God, that they are an important part of our Christian liturgy, and that the moral discourse of the deutero-Pauline epistles was directed to those who were settling into life in the real world. That real world was different from ours, but it was also different from the social world of Jesus.

In reading through the hortatory sections of the deutero-Pauline epistles, it is important to recall that their moral exhortation ("paraenesis") was designed for and directed to people who were settling into the real world. It is equally important to remember that the real world into which first century Christians settled is no longer the real world of today. Just as Christians of that era needed a new culturally conditioned response to the preaching of the gospel, so we need an ever new culturally conditioned response to the gospel in the world in which we live.

A striking example of the matter-of-fact approach to life to be found in the deutero-Pauline epistles is the profile of episcopal qualities listed in 1 Timothy 3:2-4. Having described the office of bishop as a noble task, the author lists the qualities which a bishop ought to have.[88] The bishop should be irreproachable, married only once, temperate, self-controlled, decent, hospitable, able to teach, not a drunkard, not aggressive, but gentle, not contentious, nor a lover of money. He must manage his own household well and keep his children under control with perfect dignity.

This is an impressive list of desirable qualities. One can only hope that these qualities be found in one's husband, one's neighbor, one's employer, and one's employees. They are simply the qualities to be found in a "good person" or the "upright citizen." What the author of the pastorals is saying about the bishop is that he must be a man who is well-regarded, and rightly so, in the community in which he is to minister.

Today we might retain the list. Given the state of the discipline in force in Roman Catholicism, we would delete the references about wife and family. We would probably add references to knowledge and education, to competence and pastoral skills, but the basic list would remain the same. We want all of our leaders, and especially the leaders in our church, to be persons of good character, well thought of by the community which they are called to serve.

The Sunday lectionary does not make use of 1 Timothy's list of the qualities expected to be found in someone who aspires to the office of bishop.[89] Consequently, it need not detain us any further. The passage does, however, illustrate well just how down-to-earth, matter-of-fact, and day-to-day are the ethical concerns of the deutero-Pauline literature.

The Epistle to the Ephesians

The homilist should bear this in mind when reflecting on the liturgy's use of the epistle to the Ephesians. This epistle is, as has already been noted, the most fully exploited for liturgical purposes of any of the New Testament's apostolic writings.

Scholars commonly divide the epistle to the Ephesians into two parts. Part one, the first three chapters, contains exposition or doctrine. Part two, the final three chapters, contains ethical exhortation and/or moral instruction. On the seventeenth to the twenty-first Sundays in ordinary time (Year B), that is, on five successive Sundays, the liturgical readings are taken from part two of this epistle.

The Seventeenth Sunday of Year B (Eph 4:1-6)

The reading for the seventeenth Sunday (Eph 4:1-6) describes the Christian life in terms of humility, gentleness, patience, mutual forbearance, and striving for unity. This description portrays the kinder and more gentle sort of life for which so many people strive. These qualities are requisite for life in community. Specifically, they are qualities requisite for life in that community which is the church, be it the church universal, the local church, or the domestic church.[90]

The passage appeals to the memory of Paul, the prisoner (Eph 4:1). The apostle was already dead by the time the epistle was written. Its reference to Paul's being in prison is a way of suggesting that the apostle could be not physically present to the community.[91] The invocation of the apostle's name—name-dropping, as it were—proclaims that the kind of community to whose upbuilding the apostle had devoted his entire life remains, even after his death, an ideal for which Christians must strive.

Does one need more than the memory of Paul to be motivated to live in this fashion? If so, one might remember that the church is one, holy, Catholic, and apostolic. What does it mean for the church to be one?

The reading for the seventeenth Sunday of the year recalls our hope of being one in the Lord and sharing a common destiny, a foreshadowing of which life in the church is intended to be. There is our common faith and that we have all been baptized into the single body of Christ. Our striving for unity stems from the baptism which binds us to one another and to Christ. There is but one body and one Spirit, one Lord and one God, one faith and one hope, and one baptism. In its appeal for unity within the Christian community, the reading for this eighteenth Sunday recalls the reading from 1 Corinthians 12 on the feast of Pentecost.

The Eighteenth Sunday of Year B (Eph 4:17, 20-24)

On the following Sunday the reading from Ephesians (Eph 4:17, 20-24) describes the Christian life as an ongoing conversion. It contrasts the Christian life with the life of those who have not experienced Jesus the Christ. This might give the homilist cause to reflect on the distinctiveness of the Christian way of life. Perhaps it is the occasion to recall that we are called to ever greater vitality in living the Christian life. These are not themes for Lent alone; they are aspects of the Christian life to which all Christians are called, even in "ordinary time."

The author's appeal to the Christian community is both formal and authoritative: "I declare and testify in the Lord," he writes. The homilist should not overlook the indication of the authority on the basis of which the biblical writer articulates the moral demand. "In the Lord" is not a trite formula. Coming at the beginning of an ethical appeal, as it does, it evokes the authority that the Lord has over those who acknowledge him.

People who live in our contemporary society have no lived experience of the imperial lords of ancient times nor do they have any real feeling for the medieval lords of the manor and those who served as their serfs. Today we can hardly begin to appreciate what the appeal to the Lord evoked for those who first listened to the reading of this passage. Yet today we continue to confess Jesus as our Lord and savior. And today we must strive to reflect in our personal, social, and professional lives that Jesus is Lord, the one who has dominion over all.

The goal of Christian conversion is the new person[92] created in the image of God. It is human existence such as God had intended it to be from the moment of creation. It is humanity in the fullness of what it means to be human. The author of the epistle to the Ephesians cites righteousness and holiness as qualities of this fullness of humanity. They reflect God in whose image human beings are created. It is a matter of justice and living under the influence of the Holy Spirit. The actions of Christian men and women should be in conformity with God's way of dealing with humankind.

The Nineteenth Sunday of Year B (Eph 4:30–5:2)

The nineteenth Sunday of the year is one of those occasions when the liturgical lection bridges the divide established by Stephen Langton's thirteenth century division of the New Testament into its various chapters.

The reading of Eph 4:30–5:2 rehearses elements of the readings of the two previous weeks. From the seventeenth week's lection comes the theme of kindness and compassion. Now there comes the bite. Mutual forgiveness is identified as a requisite for Christian community. This is the forgiveness for which Christians pray when they come together in liturgical assembly and recite the Lord's Prayer as their common utterance. In the Sunday's reading bitterness, fury, anger, shouting, reviling, and malice are identified as realities which destroy Christian community.

A homily is not the occasion to show one's expertise in family counseling, but anyone who works in the pastoral field knows full well—and it is the experience of all married couples—that the negative qualities cited in Ephesians 4:31 are powerful factors which impair and destroy relationships. They undermine the possibility of a marriage relationship's ability to be the foundation stone of the domestic church.[93] They prevent the family which suffers from them from being the Christian community and domestic church that it is called to be according to our vision of God's plan of salvation.

The reading for this nineteenth Sunday of the year also recalls the previous week's reading from Ephesians (Eph 4:17, 20-24) with its notion of the imitation of God, in whose image and likeness all people have been created, but adds the bite. Christians are exhorted to forgive and to love—as God forgives and loves. How difficult it is for us to forgive one another! How difficult it is for spouses to forgive the failings of their mates! And how many marriages have failed, not so much because of the fault of one spouse, as because of the inability of the other to forgive![94]

The author of Ephesians cites the forgiveness that has been realized in Christ and the love that he showed as expressions of God's forgiveness and love. What a challenge for those who realize that they are called to image God's forgiveness and love! What a consolation it is to realize that the Spirit who was operative in the first creation is likewise operative in the creation of the new person!

The Twentieth Sunday of Year B (Eph 5:15-20)

The reading appointed for the twentieth Sunday of the year (Eph 5:15-20) serves as a reminder that life in the real world is not easy. Ignorance and chemical dependence are destructive of the quality of an individual's human life. They are, moreover, blights on our society.

The author of Ephesians was not like the ostrich, with head in the sand. The author was a realist who knew full well what life in the real world was like. In the real world in which he lived, ignorance and addiction to alcohol were among the things which prevented people from realizing their human dignity and their Christian vocation. In that respect, society in late first century Ephesus is not much different from society in the late twentieth century United States.

The homilist need not and should not harangue. There is a need for sensitivity toward people who are struggling with their own ignorance or with their personal addictions. Yet, what an opportunity this reading provides for homiletic reflection on the evil of ignorance and the culpably erroneous conscience! What an opportunity to preach on alcoholism and drugs! What an occasion to speak out prophetically against social indifference to the need for general and moral education! What an occasion to recall that the wars against alcoholism and drugs are not being won! What a time to commend those individuals and social policies that are dispelling ignorance! What a time to praise individuals and groups that do their utmost to deal with the realities of chemical dependence in all their various ramifications!

Life is not entirely bleak. Moral evils are not the only reality in life. Nor should they be the sole, or even the principal, preoccupation of a homilist.[95] There is another side to life. The secularist might call it a bit of comic relief, but it is real nonetheless. That is the human relationship with God in the midst of the human struggle with one's own self.

If there is struggle in a real Christian life, there is also time for prayer. The author of Ephesians commends the singing of psalms and hymns to the Lord. He urges that thanks be addressed to God, always and for everything.

The reading for the twentieth Sunday of the year suggests so many themes for homiletic reflection. The good homilist will dwell on one. It might not be amiss for an occasional homilist to seize the epistolographer's commendation of common praise to the Lord to speak about the value of worship without the sacrament of the eucharist.

Small groups coming together for prayer and parishes that celebrate the liturgy of the hours on days when there is no priest available for the celebration of the eucharist are the experience of many Roman Catholics in the United States at the present time. So too are "priestless" parishes—and there are very many of them—that come together for worship on a regular basis despite the absence of a duly ordained priest. Before the situation of any particular community becomes critical "because there are not enough priests" to go around, a good pastor might reflect with his congregation how good and how truly a grace-filled experience it can be when Christians come together simply to praise God.

As for thanksgiving, hardly enough can be said. The church in the United States has done well to celebrate Thanksgiving as it has been celebrated in so many of our parishes during the past few years. Giving thanks should not, however, be restricted to but once a year. Giving thanks should be, as the author to the Ephesians said so well, "always and for everything" (Eph 5:20). As individuals and as communities—families, parishes, country—we have been given so much for which to be thankful. And how easy it is to forget!

Wives Should Be Submissive to Their Husbands

The reading for the twenty-first Sunday of the year (Eph 5:21-32) is really provocative. As I preside at the eucharist, I generally look out at the congregation so as to maintain eye contact with the people. As I listen to the reader proclaim that "wives should be submissive to their husbands" (Eph 5:22), the community of St. Luke's in Barrington that is so somnolent on a hot summer's day comes to life with glances, raised eyebrows, and gentle pokes-in-the-ribs—even giggling on the part of some of the younger folks. There is a similar reaction when the comparable reading from the epistle to the Colossians (Col 3:12-21)[96] is proclaimed to the congregation on the solemnity of the Holy Family.

The stirring of a congregation on a Sunday morning is not the only reaction to this lection. I remember well a particular Sunday morning when I was in the sacristy preparing for the celebration of the eucharist. The husband and wife team that had been assigned to do the readings came into the sacristy to examine the readings for the day. He looked over the reading from Joshua 24 and was relieved to find that there was nothing more difficult to pronounce than "Shechem." She began to look over the reading from Ephesians, but soon announced that he, not she, was going to have to do "that reading."

That woman's reaction is typical of that of many an educated woman and wife in today's society. They are uncomfortable with a reading that seems to relegate married women to second class status, and to do so on divine authority. The apostle Paul takes the rap for writing in a fashion which so many perceive to be misogynist when, in fact, it was not he himself who wrote these words. Be this as it may, the liturgical reading of these passages has provoked so much discussion, confusion and consternation that the bishops of the United States have petitioned Roman authorities for permission to substitute a shorter reading from Ephesians 5:25-33 on the twenty-first Sunday of the year.

At the same time, the bishops asked that a shortened reading of Colossians 3:12-17 be allowed as a pastoral option on the solemnity of the Holy Family. This reading from the epistle to the Colossians on the solemnity of the Holy Family is not quite as problematic as it once was. The second edition of the editio typ-ica of the *Order of Readings for Mass* now provides for different readings from the apostolic writings when the solemnity of the Holy Family is celebrated in years B and C.[97]

A Literary Form

Exercising the pastoral option of substituting the shorter read-ing of Colossians and Ephesians for the longer may be a matter of winning the battle but losing the war. Choosing a shorter read-ing allows those who prepare the Sunday liturgy to omit a prob-lematic passage of scripture. Exercising this option does not, however, remove the verse from the scriptures nor does it erase the knowledge of that scripture from people's consciousness. "Cleaning up the readings" in this fashion does not address the broader pastoral concern of those who are really troubled by the fact that our scriptures have affirmed that wives should be sub-missive to their husbands. Nor does it address the fact that some fundamentalists take the verse as "the gospel truth" and seek to create a society in which women are really submissive to men.

Part of the problem posed by the lectionary's text selection is that on the twenty-first Sunday of Year B and on the solemnity of the Holy Family the lectionary's editors have chosen for the litur-gical reading of the day only part of pertinent scriptural topos

(Eph 5:21-32; Col 3:12-21). They have omitted Ephesians 6:1-9 (and Col 3:22-25) from the public reading of the text, thereby taking these verses out of the context to which they belong. Reading the scriptural text as the lectionary presents it, even in the longer version, is somewhat similar to reading a miracle story, but omitting from the story any mention of healing or a description of the ailment. The truncated reading does not respect the literary form of the passage written by one of Paul's disciples.[98] Back in the thirteenth century, when Stephen Langton divided the New Testament into our present-day chapters, people were not aware of the importance of the bible's literary forms. Langton concluded the fifth chapter of Ephesians at verse 33 and the third chapter of Colossians at verse 25.

When we read the biblical text without the distraction caused by Langton's division of the chapters, we easily recognize that the scriptural units are, respectively, Ephesians 5:21–6:9 and Colossians 3:18–4:1. These two passages have a common structure; they present what biblical scholars call a household code or a household table.[99] Ephesians has a somewhat longer version of the code than does Colossians, but a common structure is present in both texts.[100] Many scholars consider that the text of Ephesians is literarily dependent on that of Colossians. In any case, when the household code of Ephesians (Eph 5:21–6:9) is compared with that of Colossians (Col 3:18–4:1), the text of Ephesians appears to be a much fuller and more complex reflection on the basic structure than does what Colossians has to say about it.[101]

The structure essentially focuses on order in the first century Hellenistic household. Three sets of social relationships are presented: the husband-wife relationship, the parent-child relationship, and the master-slave relationship. These essential relationships characterized life in the typical household of that society.

In their concern for order within the household—what household does not need some order?—our versions of the household code first present the situation of those whom first century society considered to be socially inferior in the various household relationships, wives, children, and slaves. These are respectively exhorted to obey their husbands, parents, and masters. Thereafter, the household code addresses the situation of those whom society considered to be socially superior. They were exhorted to treat their "inferior" partners appropriately. Thus husbands were urged to love their wives, fathers not to provoke their children, and masters to treat their slaves fairly.

The reference to slaves and masters (Eph 6:5-9; Col 3:22–4:1), and the patriarchalism inherent in an exhortation addressed to fathers—but not to mothers!—not to provoke their children (Eph 6:4; Col 3:21), are two indications of just how culturally conditioned these expressions of the household code truly are. On neither the twenty-first Sunday of the year nor on the solemnity of the Holy Family does the liturgical lection include that portion of the household code which deals with slaves and masters (Eph 6:5-9; Col 3:22–4:1). The lectionary's cropping of the household code at Ephesians 5:32 (and at Colossians 3:21) is a liturgical recognition of the fact that the social conditions which led to the scriptures' incorporation of household codes[102] are no longer the social conditions which exist today.

The household code makes use of a very old literary form. Its origins go back to Aristotle. The traditional exhortation was widely echoed by Hellenistic moralists, particularly those belonging to the Stoic and Cynic philosophical traditions. As an expression of the accepted wisdom, the household code entered into Hellenistic Judaism. Thereafter it was appropriated by Hellenistic Christianity. It did, after all, represent how the people of those Hellenistic times thought a well-run household should function.

Use of a household code by early Christian authors was particularly appropriate in the late first and early second centuries. At that time Christians were accused of being disruptive of the social order. On the political scene, they refused obeisance to divinized emperors. On the domestic scene, various women, young people, and slaves had become Christian. Such phenomena led to widespread social suspicion of Christians and even to the persecution of Christians, considered to be people who disrupted social order and disturbed domestic harmony. In those circumstances the use of the household code was a way for Christians to affirm that they accepted the family values then in vogue.

The Household Code Today

Does it make any sense for the church of the present day to preserve the reading of the household code in its liturgy? I think that it does. It makes sense to read the household code in the socially conditioned formulation which we hear in the biblical texts, precisely because it is a socially conditioned formulation. Families do not exist except within the structures of the cultural conditions of their own time and place. The acultural family is unreal; it simply does not exist. It is an abstraction, the figment of imagination.

By presenting the well-ordered household as an element of its paraenesis our biblical tradition affirms, as it were, that God has an interest in family life as it is actually lived. One cannot make of any given society's family structures the norm for all families of all times and places. We can, however, affirm that God is not indifferent to family life, as it is actually structured within any given society. That the New Testament's household codes point to an historically and socially conditioned structure of the family is not a liability; it is an asset, because it points to God's concern for the real family rather than for an ideal or abstract family.

The historically and socially conditioned household code suggests that one must live one's Christian vocation in and through one's social relationships. These social relationships are historically conditioned. One must live one's life-in-family within the family such as it actually exists. How one relates to the members of one's family is an image of one's relationship with God; it is a way of living out our relationship with God. That is so clear, especially in the letter to the Ephesians, whose author—almost in an aside—reflects, "This is a great mystery.[103] I mean that it refers to Christ and the church" (Eph 5:32).

The Basic Message

When a reading of the household code is found in the scriptures or assigned for liturgical reading, its basic message should not be overlooked. The basic message of the household code per se is that some order and structure are necessary in order for a family to function well. This is a truism, but one that is often overlooked, if not neglected, because of individuals' pursuing their own agenda even within the family unit.

By adding that love should characterize a man's relationship with his wife, that religious formation should be part of parents' concern for their children, and that all of us are ultimately responsible to the one Lord, the household code of Ephesians teaches that there ought to be something distinctive about a Christian family. The presence of this household code in the scriptures and its use in our Sunday liturgy remind us that a concern that each family of Christians be truly a Christian family has ever been and continues to be a concern of the church. The well-being of the families who belong to the church is important for the well-being of the church itself.

Over the course of the centuries, family structures have changed considerably, but there is more than a little gnomic wisdom in the notion that children should obey their parents and that parents should not provoke their children. This is simply a matter of common sense.

On the other hand, the two-pronged exhortation to slaves and masters, that slaves should obey their masters and that masters should treat their slaves fairly, when taken with naive literalism, is no longer pertinent to our times. Every householder, nonetheless, expects that employees, even those as temporary as someone who has been called to repair the television set in the living room, will come on time and that they will do the job for which they have been hired. We are upset when repairers do not show up at the agreed time. We would certainly be justified were we to react negatively to a repairer who had signed a contract to repair a faulty refrigerator, but who, on arrival, insists on working on the television rather than on the refrigerator that stands in need of repair.

Conversely, people who are called to someone's house to do some repairs can legitimately expect to be paid justly and in timely fashion. They have every right to be properly treated. They have every right, in the words of the household code, to be treated impartially (Eph 6:9), that is, justly and fairly (Col 4:1).

Although there are manifest differences between the economic structures of late twentieth century America and those of the first century Hellenistic world, there is no little analogy between the situation of those who expected work to be done and those who did the expected work in ancient times and today's expectations vis-à-vis the work force. The analogy allows the reading and exposition of this section of the household code to continue to have significance for people of today.

Situated in Time and Space

In a sense the temporal situation to which the household code refers is at once its strength and its liability. It is its strength insofar as it recalls that one must live the Christian life within the context of a socially conditioned set of human relationships. It becomes a liability when one attempts to make the social relationships of yesteryear a norm for the social relationships of today.

When preaching the household codes the homilist should not proclaim that wives should be submissive to their husbands. Such submission is no longer culturally acceptable; indeed, in our times, it may well be antithetical to the gospel itself. On the other hand, the liturgical reading of the household code may provide a pastorally sensitive homilist with an opportune occasion for reflecting on the changing nature of the family structure.

All too often we presume that the nuclear family, with two parents, is the time-honored norm. Those who give normative status to this "typical American family" may well regret and bemoan our changing family structures, particularly the single parent family. We bewail the demise of "family values." In fact, the type of family that many consider to be the norm (or ideal!) is a relative newcomer on the human scene. Most societies in the past, and many that continue to exist in the present, consider the extended family to be the basic social structure and the fundamental unit of society. The recent American version of a nuclear family system lacks many of the strengths of the extended family system. Indeed there are social scientists who question whether our "traditional" nuclear family structure is as strong as many have naively presumed it to be.

As a matter of fact, the traditional family structure, at least in the form in which it existed in the United States in the earlier decades of this century, may not be as traditional as many think it to be. The Quaker, child-centered family of the middle colonies has become our national bourgeois norm. During the seventeenth and eighteenth centuries it was primarily American fathers who had the primary responsibility for child care beyond the early nursing period.

Reflections on facts such as these should make the homilist realize just how atypical is the type of family existence that many Americans idealize. The "typical" twentieth century white American family can hardly be considered as the perennial norm for family structure. The household code reminds us that God has an interest in human families and that those who live in human families are to respond to God's call within the vicissitudes of real human families. These always exist in a rather particular set of social circumstances.

The household code reminds us that the human family has a history and a story. It may also remind us that our God is the Lord of history and the God of the living.

8

Today's Church

Since the beginning of Vatican Council II various conciliar and post-conciliar documents have reminded us of the exceptional place which the scripturally-based liturgical homily should have in the life and prayer of the church and its members. In response to the council's call for a richer fare of scriptural passages to be offered to the faithful, the order of readings for Sundays and solemnities presently lists about two hundred passages from the New Testament's apostolic writings.

The previous chapter offered a few reflections as to how the semi-continuous reading of the epistle to the Ephesians on the Sundays of ordinary time in Year B might serve as a useful basis for homiletic exposition. In a book as short as this, it is impossible to pass in review all of the Sunday lectionary's list of liturgical readings. I will, nonetheless, cite a few other passages as examples of the homiletic use to which the (second) scriptural readings of Sunday can be put. For the most part, these will be readings whose homiletic exposition might be of particular value for the people of St. Catherine's parish in Mountain Lakes, but which might easily be passed over. The themes to which I will point are matters of relevant topicality and of particular urgency for the church today.

Year C
The Twelfth Sunday of Year C (Gal 3:26-29)

On the twelfth Sunday of the year, the scriptural readings come from Zechariah 12:10-11, Luke 9:18-24 and Galatians 3:26-29. In the presence of the very powerful Lukan tale of Jesus' interrogation of his disciples on the subject of his own identity and status, the reading from Galatians may easily be overlooked.

Although the Lukan story of Jesus' dialogue with his disciples has its own distinctive features, its Matthean and Markan parallels were read on previous Sundays of the three year cycle. Matthew 16:13-20 was read on the twenty-first Sunday of Year A and Mark 8:27-35 on the twenty-fourth Sunday of Year B. One can presume that these gospel lections served as the basis for the homily on the respective Sundays. In contrast, the reading from Galatians 3:26-29 occurs only in Year C. It does not have any immediate parallel, to be read on some other occasion during the three year cycle of liturgical readings. Galatians 3:26-29 is a very important piece of the Christian scriptures, one that deserves exposition, especially at the present time.[104] Thus it could be quite useful for a preacher at St. Catherine's to forego a homily on the Lukan text in order to preach on Paul's message to the churches of Galatia for the benefit of the church in Mountain Lakes.

The baptismal formula cited by Paul recalls that "there does not exist male or female" for we are all one in Christ Jesus. Paul's words make obvious reference to the creation story of Genesis 1:27.[105] Today his words serve almost as a slogan in much of Christian feminist hermeneutics.[106] In Mountain Lakes, Paul's words provide the Sunday homilist with an opportunity—and the challenge!—to talk about the role of women in the church.

They also provide a homilist with a summer time's opportunity to preach about baptism. In recent years, various elements of Paul's baptismal reflection have been incorporated into the church's baptismal catechesis. The themes of faith, becoming children of God, being united to Christ, and being one in Christ come immediately to mind. Less obvious, though likewise important as a baptismal theme, is the idea that the unity-in-diversity of the church is a sign of our unity-in-diversity in Christ, itself a sacramental sign of the kingdom of God.[107]

Although Paul has specifically written about Jew and Greek, slave and free, male and female, his words draw attention to the classic ethnic, social, and gender-related divisions that separate humans from one another. Paul's baptismal observations can provide a homilist with an opportunity to rehearse some aspects of the ever important Jewish-Christian dialogue for the benefit of the congregation which gathers in Mountain Lakes. Alternatively they can force us to think about ethnic prejudice, racist attitudes, and the need for racial and ethnic complementarity in the human community.

The apostle's words call us to pause and reflect on those ethnic, social, and sexual differences which separate us from one another when, instead, we are called to be one in Christ. What Paul has written invites us to think about the catholicity of the church and how that catholicity ought to function as a sign and means by which the kingdom of God is realized. Indeed, the very short passage from Paul's letter to the Galatians provides a point of departure for many a Sunday homily. His insights intersect with so many different situations in the church and in the world today.

The Fifteenth Sunday of Year C (Col 1:15-20)

The readings for the fifteenth Sunday of the year can be cited as another illustration of how the lectionary functions in ordinary time. The commandments are the common theme of the first and third readings for this Sunday, Deuteronomy 30:10-14 and Luke 10:25-27. Paul has written a midrash (that is, a scriptural commentary) on this passage from Deuteronomy 30 in Romans 10:6-10. Romans 10, however, has not been chosen as a scriptural reading for the day.[108] The New Testament reading selected for the eucharistic liturgy of the fifteenth Sunday of the year is taken from Colossians 1:15-20.

The passage is one of the most important Christological hymns in the New Testament. It succinctly expresses the basic Christology of the epistle to the Colossians.[109] It serves as the foundation for the author's reflections on suffering and on the revelation of the mystery, on baptism and new life in Christ, and on the practical realities of what it means to be a new person in Christ. Many of these themes will be further developed in the readings from the epistle to the Colossians which will follow in the weeks to come (16th–18th Sundays, Year C).

Were one to categorize this magnificent hymn in terms of the present-day Christological discussion, one would say that the Christology of Colossians 1:15-20 is an early example of "Christology from above." In well-chosen words it projects the iconic image of Christ the Pantocrator. The Colossians' hymn offers a magnificent cosmic vision, yet not without recalling that its Christology from above has a soteriological interest. This is important for the New Testament authors. Their vision of God and his Christ is not so much concerned with questions of divine identity and philosophical inquiry as it is concerned with the salvific relationship between God and humankind.

The reading of the Colossians' Christological hymn during the celebration of Sunday eucharist might give an enterprising homilist an occasion on which to speak to the congregation about the development of Christology, whether in the early church or in the church of today. The homilist should not fail to mention that Paul's own Christology evolved as he interacted with real groups of people whose situations, with their challenges and questions, led the apostle to an ever deeper understanding of the One whom he had experienced on the road to Damascus. A preacher can make use of this hymn to reflect on the development of dogma for the good of the church which gathers at St. Matthias' in Lanham.

The reading of the Christological hymn from the epistle to the Colossians is the first of the four readings from this epistle, appointed for semi-continuous reading in Year C. Should a homilist choose to preach on the hymn on the fifteenth Sunday of the year, he or she should follow through by continuing to use the epistle to the Colossians as the basis for one's homily in the weeks to come. The homiletic exposition of the Christological hymn of Colossians 1:15-20 provides a good start.

The Twenty-Fourth Sunday of Year C (1 Tim 1:12-17)

The proclamation of Colossians' Christological hymn on the fifteenth Sunday of Year C is the first of a twenty-week-long series of readings from the deutero-Pauline literature, interrupted only by a short passage from the letter to Philemon on the twenty-third Sunday.

On the twenty-fourth Sunday of the year, the lectionary presents us with a marvelous portrayal of St. Paul (1 Tim 1:12-17). The lectionary's Paul is the Paul of Christian tradition. It is not a self-portrait; rather it is a portrait of the apostle, sketched by an unknown disciple. The writer deliberately portrays a picture of Paul as someone whom we should imitate: "an example to those who would later have faith."

The Paul of the author's imagination is the greatest of sinners and the greatest of saints. As we continue to look at the image which the author has portrayed, a homilist might choose to reflect on what Saint Paul has meant for the Christian tradition. Otherwise, the Sunday preacher might chose to discourse on the imitation of the saints, perhaps even on more recent saints, canonized or not, whose example can serve to edify people today. Stylized lives of the saints once formed the heart of much catechetical instruction within Roman Catholicism. This twenty-fourth Sunday of the year provides an occasion for the example of the saints to enter once again into Christian consciousness.

Then again, the twenty-fourth Sunday of the year might be a good time for the homilist to talk about conversion, and about how all people, from the greatest to the least, from sinner to saint, need to undergo a process of conversion in their lives.

The Twenty-Fifth Sunday of Year C (1 Tim 2:1-8)

On the following Sunday, the twenty-fifth of the year, the lector continues the reading of the first epistle to Timothy. The passage fills in the stylized portrayal of Paul the apostle, now described as preacher, apostle, and teacher of the Gentiles in faith and in truth. Preacher, apostle and teacher are three different but related functions enjoyed by Paul. He was someone who preached the gospel of God. As an apostle, he had been sent to the Gentiles and had founded communities of believers, churches, in various communities of the Gentiles. He remains a teacher for all those Gentiles, us moderns included, who read his letters and learn from his example.

Nonetheless, it is on prayer that the lesson of this twenty-fifth Sunday of the year concentrates its attention. Occasionally one finds in the literature on the pastoral epistles the suggestion that 1 Timothy 2:1-8 is a remnant of a eucharistic prayer. This suggestion is overly specific, but the reading chosen for this twenty-fifth Sunday clearly proffers guidelines for praying in public and makes the claim that these guidelines are in keeping with apostolic tradition, that they were promulgated on the basis of Paul's apostolic authority. The document from which the reading is taken has the form of the apostolic constitutions; it is almost a primitive compendium of the canon law of the church.

A homilist at St. Joseph's in Grand Rapids would not be off-target were he or she to seize the occasion offered by this twenty-fifth Sunday to instruct and motivate the congregation with regard to its common prayer. The reading of 1 Timothy 2:1-8 might provide a good occasion for a much needed instruction on proper liturgical practice. Alternatively, a reminder that prayers of the faithful ought to be general intercessions would not be far off the mark. The text insists that prayer be offered for everyone, including all those in authority. Its explanation focuses on the fact that there is but one God and a single mediator for all.

That an emphatic "all" occurs three times in the passage is due to the fact that the epistle was written at a time when gnostic elitism was threatening the Christian congregation. Even today Christians have a tendency to limit the scope of their prayers. They commonly pray for their friends, co-religionists, and the citizens of their own country. The lection from 1 Timothy serves as a sharp reminder that Christian intercessory prayer embraces all.[110]

As important as is community prayer, it is also important that those who pray in community have the proper disposition. In the words of Paul's disciple, they must be blameless, free from anger and dissension. Anger and dissension disrupt life in community. The one who prays in community should be communitarian in disposition. This rejoinder is in keeping with the prophetic dictum that God wants love, not sacrifice (Hos 6:6; cf. Mark 12:33).

The Twenty-Ninth Sunday of Year C (2 Tim 3:14–4:2)

A few Sundays later, on the twenty-ninth Sunday of the year, the scripture lesson from the apostolic writings is 2 Timothy 3:14–4:2. The passage provides our tradition with its formal biblical foundation for the doctrine of inspiration: "all scripture is inspired of God and is useful for teaching—for reproof, correction, and training in holiness."

In face of the pastoral crisis provoked by widespread biblical fundamentalism, the reading of this passage of scripture provides one who preaches at Our Lady of Refuge in Castroville with a good opportunity to talk to the congregation about the nature of inspiration and the role of the scriptures in the church.[111] Indeed the pastoral situation of the church today might lead to the conclusion that a homilist does not have an option in this regard. The situation is so serious that all who share in the pastoral responsibility for a parish have a weighty pastoral responsibility to talk to the congregation about the scriptures and their inspiration.

The passage from 2 Timothy continues with the exhortation "to preach the word." The epistles to Timothy are addressed to a typical church leader, as represented by Timothy. The exhortation contained in 2 Timothy 4:1-2 was presumably intended for church leaders. As the church becomes ever more aware of the ecclesial responsibility of all the baptized, the reading of this passage from scripture provides a good opportunity for a reflection on evangelization. Paul VI's apostolic exhortation, *Evangelii nuntiandi*, and John Paul II's call for a new evangelization remind us of the responsibility of every Christian to participate personally in the church's mission of evangelization. It is a responsibility which cannot be delegated to a few.

Year A
The Fourth Sunday of Advent (Rom 1:1-7)

Advent's apostolic readings consist of various exhortations and proclamations which are thematically united with different Advent motifs. The reading appointed for the fourth Sunday of Advent is the beginning of Paul's letter to the Romans. The link between Romans 1:1-7 and the other readings selected for the day, Isaiah 7:10-14 and Matthew 1:18-24, is readily apparent. All three scriptures focus on the house of David, thereby drawing the Christian congregation's attention to the messianic dignity of the One whose birth is about to be celebrated.

The theme is so blatant that a homilist should not too readily depart from it. Nonetheless, the preacher might recall that, in the judgment of many scholars, the beginning of Paul's letter to the Romans incorporates an excerpt from an early Christian creed which proclaimed the double sonship of Jesus: he "was descended from David according to the flesh but was made Son of God in power, according to the spirit of holiness, by his resurrection from the dead." Jesus Christ is, as we so often hear during the celebration of the liturgy of the Christmas season, "Son of God and son of Mary." The creed which the congregation affirms as it gathers each Sunday proclaims that Jesus was "born of the Virgin Mary and became man." This is the mystery of the incarnation, of the Word become flesh.

As the Christmas season approaches, a homilist might well decide to focus on the function of the creed in the Christian community. We recognize one another as Christians by the common faith which we profess. The Christians of Rome recognized Paul by the creed which he professed as he began his letter to them. That creed proclaimed that Jesus was "descended from David according to the flesh but was made Son of God in power, according to the spirit of holiness." The Nicean creed professes that Jesus Christ is the only Son of God, eternally begotten of the Father, who by the power of the Holy Spirit was born of the Virgin Mary and became man. This double confession of faith may well serve as the leitmotif of a pre-Christmas homily.

More about the Sundays of Easter

Human suffering is, and has always been, a mystery. The suffering of human beings is one of the great problems of theodicy, as the holocaust of Auschwitz and the famine in the Horn of Africa continue hauntingly to remind us. While humankind must confront suffering on a cosmic level, individuals have to come to grips with suffering in their own lives and the lives of those whom they love. What to do about suffering? How do we make sense of it? How do we cope with it? No one has the answer, but we do need to talk about it.[112]

Discourse on human suffering is a very difficult discourse to conduct. The homilist must avoid every semblance of a non-Christian fatalism, as if suffering were simply inevitable. He or she must be careful to avoid extolling suffering as if it were a human good, an end in itself. Dealing with the sufferings of Jesus, one must be careful to avoid a kind of dramatization that would unduly concentrate on the intensity of Jesus' suffering rather than on the mystery of salvation.[113]

Despite these difficulties, the fact remains that human suffering is a painful part of our individual, corporate, and global experience. None of us escapes from the reality of suffering. Accordingly, it behooves pastors and other preachers to address this issue which so grips the members of the congregation to the very depths of their being.

The readings from the first letter of Peter on the second (1 Pet 1:3-9), fourth (1 Pet 2:20-25), sixth (1 Pet 3:15-18), and seventh (1 Pet 4:13-16) Sundays of Easter time present homilists with opportunities to reflect on the enigma of human suffering. The example of Jesus and the perspective provided by the resurrection put human suffering into a meaningful context. The message of hope provided by the resurrection challenges the preacher to talk about human suffering in a meaningful and faithful way.

When we realize just how often the theme of human suffering occurs in the readings of the Easter season (Year A), we are reminded of the importance of looking ahead and planning our homilies in a comprehensive fashion. Those who plan ahead may choose to divide the question of human suffering when the text at hand is the first epistle of Peter. The second Sunday of Easter, that is, the Sunday after Easter, provides an occasion for the homilist to recall that Jesus' resurrection and our faith provide the perspective from which to view all aspects of human life, including the mystery of human suffering. The fourth Sunday is one on which we can recall the meaning of Jesus' sufferings, and that no disciple is above the master. On the sixth Sunday, we can turn our attention to hope in the midst of suffering, or counter the claim that only the guilty should suffer, or remark that we ought not to suffer because of our indiscretions.

Alternatively, the latter theme might be reserved for the seventh Sunday of Easter. Then again, the homily for the seventh Sunday of Easter might take the Petrine beatitude as its point of departure. "Happy are you when you are insulted for the sake of Christ, for then God's Spirit in its glory has come to rest on you" (1 Pet 4:14) recalls the last beatitude in the synoptics' collection, blessed are those who are persecuted for Jesus' sake (Matt 5:10-12; Luke 6:22). The reading appointed for this final Sunday in Easter time is one which proclaims that the suffering of the righteous is a prelude to their beatitude. This is the eschatological reversal that is characteristic of the coming of the kingdom of God.

The Thirty-Third Sunday of Year C

A reading from 2 Thessalonians 3:7-12 occurs on the thirty-third Sunday of Year C, the end of the three year cycle of liturgical readings. It is followed by the celebration of the feast of Christ the King. Then the church begins its new year, with a reading from Romans 13:11-14 on the first Sunday of Advent in Year A.

Without knowing the strategic location of this passage from 2 Thessalonians in the church's course of readings, many use its exhortation as a quip: "Anyone who would not work should not eat" (v. 10). Work is, nonetheless, a very significant part of life and a very important human value. It is particularly valued in the Judeo-Christian tradition because God has confided the care of the created universe to men and women, as both the story of creation in Genesis 1 and the fourth eucharistic prayer continually remind us.

In his first letter to the Thessalonians, Paul proudly recalled that he and his companions had "worked night and day" during the time of their visit to the Thessalonians (1 Thess 2:9). In that letter, Paul asked the Thessalonians not to forget his labor and toil. Now, in another address to the Thessalonians, Paul's anonymous disciple presents Paul's heartfelt work as an example to be emulated. Working is a way of sharing stewardship over all creation. Insofar as providing for oneself is a way not to burden others, working to support oneself and one's family can also be seen as an expression of Christian charity. Doing one's fair share is an exercise in responsibility toward the community, large or small, to which one belongs.

Homilists sometimes preach about the dignity of human labor. Typically they do so on the feast of Joseph the Worker or on Labor Day weekend.[114] The appearance of 2 Thessalonians 3:7-12 in the lectionary provides yet another and meaningful occasion to talk about the dignity of human labor. In times of massive unemployment, or when there is popular resentment against public monies being spent to support a minimal livelihood for the unemployed, this next-to-last Sunday of the year might be an occasion for the preacher to reflect with his congregation on the tragic fate of those who are unable to realize their human dignity because they are out of work.

In any case, as the church uses the final Sundays of the year to reflect on the coming of the end times, and as society gets caught up in all the bustle of "the holidays," the reading of 2 Thessalonians 3:7-12 comes as a stark reminder that work is an essential element of what it means to be human and what it means to be Christian. How we work is a matter of imitating the example of the apostle Paul and his companions. Working is a way of being a responsible co-citizen within society. How we work is also a matter of responsible participation in the ongoing creation of God, whose own tale of creation is cast in the form of a story about someone at work (Gen 1).

Looking Back

Sometimes I find myself comparing the deutero-Pauline exhortation to work with Jesus' dialogue about suffering immediately after the narrative of the transfiguration.[115] It was wonderful for disciples of Jesus to have had an experience of the transcendent, but Jesus immediately reminded them that there still remained the harsher realities of life. In the celebration of the eucharistic liturgy and in our prayer together, we have an experience of God and of community. Lest we be carried away in the ecstasy of the moment, lest we, like Peter, want to hold fast to that experience forever, the reading of 2 Thessalonians comes as a reminder that we are called to get on with life, in the practicalities and the struggles of it, because God is there as well.

Preaching is a matter of letting the word of God enter into people's lives. It is a matter of allowing God's word to penetrate their very being so as to transform and vivify them.

As I look back on the extended reflection contained in this book, I am fully aware that I have touched upon only some of the passages that the church has selected for liturgical readings on the Sundays and solemnities of the year. Almost by design, I have not concentrated on those passages whose "religious message" is most apparent. Rather I have chosen to focus on those passages whose message is perhaps more secular.

I have done so because it is my experience that these passages are rarely served to the typical Sunday congregation. I have done so because of a conviction that the people of God have a right to be fed. The food with which they need to be fed is the very word of God which will equip them for life and for work with one another and in doing so will bring them closer to the God who is the source of all life and the energy for all work.

Looking Ahead

I have written this book from the perspective of one who is, by vocation, a preacher and a priest. It is also written from the perspective of one who is, by profession, a scripture scholar who has spent a good part of his adult life studying the letters of Paul and the other apostolic writings. It is primarily from this latter perspective that the following chapters have been written. They are concerned with the transformation of Paul's letters and the other apostolic letters when these texts are appropriated by the church's liturgy.

9

What Happened
to Paul's Letters:
The Place of Paul in the Liturgy

New Testament scholars occasionally write about "the lectionary text," the particular form of the New Testament text which appears in the lectionary. Almost two thousand relatively ancient Greek-language New Testament lectionaries are known to exist. For biblical scholars these lectionaries are helpful in the preparation of the modern edition of the New Testament in Greek. Specialists in the field, the text critics, are aware that the passages which have been designated for liturgical reading have been selected and edited for liturgical use. This gives them a particular configuration, called the "lectionary text."

Many of the processes and principles employed in the preparation of the biblical texts for liturgical use in the ancient church were also used in the preparation of those texts from the letters and other apostolic writings which are appointed for public reading during our celebration of the Sunday eucharist. Accordingly it is appropriate to speak about our own "lectionary text" of the New Testament epistles.[116]

Translation

Greater participation by the laity in the worship of the church was one of the most important aims of the liturgical reform initiated by the Second Vatican Council. To achieve this end, the biblical texts proclaimed in liturgical celebrations are generally read in one of our modern languages. Any translation of an ancient text into a modern language implies that the linguistic structures of the modern language impose themselves upon the translated text. This is a given. It applies to the translation of the biblical texts as well as to the translation of classical authors.

When translations are made with liturgical usage in mind,[117] the translators need to be attentive to additional dynamics. A translator who is preparing a text for use in the liturgy must pay attention to the general appropriateness of the text in a liturgical setting. Particular attention must be given, for example, to the rhythm of sentences and the sound of words. Sentences that are too long and words that are tongue-twisters are not appropriate for a translation that is to be read in public worship.

Inclusive Language

In our day many people are offended when they hear the reading of "brothers" when the scriptures are proclaimed during the liturgy. "Brothers" is the literal translation of *adelphoi*, a formula of direct address used by Paul and other apostolic authors to appeal directly to their audience and engage them in conversation. Today, instead of engaging the hearers in what Paul had to say, "brothers" distances people from the Pauline appeal. Paul's message, addressed to "brothers," appears to have been for another time and place. Alternatively, "brothers" appears to make Paul's words a message for men only. People feel left out, demeaned, or annoyed when they hear "brothers." Some even find Paul's words offensive. This is a serious pastoral situation, especially during the celebration of the eucharist which is intended to bring us together as one body in Christ.

Most of the recent translations of the New Testament into English, including the revised New Testament of the New American Bible (1986),[118] the New Jerusalem Bible (1985), and the New Revised Standard Version (1990), offer a different translation of Paul's *adelphoi*. Not only have they tried to avoid the sexist term, "brothers," and replace it with more inclusive language;[119]

they have also attempted to find a translation that would more adequately render the true meaning of Paul's words.

The attempt has been particularly successful in the case of the New Revised Standard Version, a translation that was made with the expressed intention of producing a text that would be suitable for liturgical reading. The Episcopal Commission for Liturgy of the Canadian Bishops' Conference chose this translation for use in its 1992 lectionary. In commending the use of this new translation, the commission's editorial note to the lectionary drew attention to the fact that the NRSV is widely used among Christians of all denominations. The editorial further recalls that the committee responsible for the translation was concerned "to make the text easier for proclamation and to employ inclusive language when the text or meaning obviously applied to both men and women."[120]

In place of the "brothers" of the older lectionaries, we now commonly hear "brothers and sisters." When the new order of readings is fully implemented, the phrase, "brothers and sisters" will be heard quite frequently. The introduction to the *New Order of Readings* urges that during the liturgy scriptural readings begin with an appropriate introductory phrase, an "incipit."[121] In the case of the letters, the suggested incipit is "brothers and sisters" or "dearly beloved." Thus, on the first Sunday of Advent in Year A, the reading from Romans 13:11-14 will begin "Brothers and sisters, you know what time it is."[122]

Even apart from the incipits soon to be added to the liturgical readings, the phrase, "brothers and sisters," occurs with some frequency in the lectionary. *Adelphoi* is one of Paul's favorite expressions, punctuating many of his letters. Paul uses the phrase as a form of direct address in all letters save one—the brief letter to Philemon, where, nonetheless, *adelphe*, the singular of the Greek form, "brother," appears in verses 7 and 20, in obvious reference to Philemon himself. "Brothers and sisters" occurs most often in Paul's letters to communities with whom he had a particularly warm and friendly relationship. Proportionately the expression is found most often in his correspondence with the Thessalonians (fourteen times) and the Philippians (seven times), but it is not absent from his first letter to the Corinthians (nineteen times).[123] On the other hand, the phrase is found only ten times in the very long letter to the Romans, a community which Paul had yet to visit at the time that he was writing his letter.[124]

Since Paul used "brothers and sisters" as often as he did, it is clear that he intended this formula to serve as a means by which he reached out to and engaged those to whom he was writing. Paul made a "fraternal" appeal to those whom he had come to experience as his brothers and sisters. His language evokes the very strong bonds that bound him to the communities which he had evangelized. It was that bonding to which he could appeal when he wanted to get his hearers caught up into what he was writing to them.

To catch fully all the nuances of Paul's use of this term, we should remember that first-generation Christians gathered in the homes of one of their number. It was in someone's home that they listened to the reading of the letters which Paul had written. In that home they celebrated the family and commemorative meal, known then as "the breaking of the bread," and known later as the eucharist. In a very real sense, the church of those early years was "at home," for it was in someone's home that believers came together for their gatherings. Family language, "brother," "sister," "mother," "father," is language that properly belongs at home. Thus when Paul addresses the Christians to whom he writes as *adelphoi* he is evoking not only the bonds between him and them, he is also evoking his own experience of Christians gathering together in someone's home, in the venue where family language truly belongs.

Recent studies have shown that in the koine Greek used in Paul's time *adelphoi* was commonly employed to address groups of men and women. "Brothers" may be its literal translation, but "brothers and sisters" is the more appropriate translation. Because "brothers and sisters" evokes not only the warm personal relationship that existed between Paul and the communities which he evangelized, but also the theological reality of our new kinship in Christ, Paul's *adelphoi* really should not be translated by a mundane "friends" or "fellow Christians." It really means "brothers and sisters."

In his letters, Paul wrote to the men and women of his churches. Men and women gathered to listen to what he had to say. He called them his brothers and sisters because of the intensity of the bonds of love which linked them together. Still today men and women gather together to listen to what Paul has written. Hopefully the bonds which tie these Christians together are as intense as were the bonds which linked the first generations of Christians with one another!

In those churches where the older lectionaries are still in use, readers might well be instructed to substitute "brothers and sisters" when the translation that lies before their eyes has only "brothers." The newer translation is not only the result of greater sensitivity to the feelings of the people of our times, it is also a matter of greater fidelity to Paul and the language which he used.

Taken Out of Context and Adapted

Passages chosen for liturgical reading have been taken out of their biblical context. They are read independently of the literary context within which they were originally written. Moreover, the passages chosen for liturgical reading are sometimes modified so that they might be more readily understood by the faithful.

Some Things Are Added

Lest the scriptural readings begin too abruptly, common introductory phrases, technically known as incipits, are often added to the beginning of the reading. Prior to the reform of the eucharistic liturgy undertaken in response to the directives of Vatican Council II, for example, Latin Rite Catholics customarily listened to a reading from one of the gospels which began with the introductory phrase, *in diebus illis* ("in those days"). This formula comes from the gospel according to Matthew.[125] It does not, however, occur at the beginning of each and every one of Matthew's little stories about Jesus. The formula is, nonetheless, a good way to begin a gospel lection which otherwise might have started too abruptly. In similar fashion, the *New Order of*

Readings suggests that "brothers and sisters" be used to intro-duce the readings from Paul's letters during our celebration of liturgy.

When the bible is read sequentially, as it normally would be by someone who reads the bible at home, the meaning of its var-ious pronouns is readily inferred from the immediate context.[126] When, however, a passage is taken out of its biblical context, as it is for liturgical usage, the antecedents for the various pronouns must be supplied in order that those who are listening to the reading really understand what they have heard. Thus the lec-tionary text frequently includes nouns—and occasionally other explanatory phrases[127]—which do not appear in the New Testament itself. These are added to the liturgical reading for clarity's sake.

On the tenth Sunday of Year A, for example, the name of Abraham has been added to the liturgical reading of Romans 4:18-25. The liturgical revisers have taken the name of our ances-tor in faith from verse 16 of Paul's letter so that the members of the congregation might more readily recognize who it was of whom Paul was writing, when he cited an example of faith for us to imitate. In similar fashion, the liturgical reading of the Christological hymn from the epistle to the Colossians on the fif-teenth Sunday of Year C begins with "Christ Jesus." Jesus is so named in verse 3 of the epistle, but not in Colossians 1:15, where the liturgical reading appointed for the day begins.

And Some Things Are Omitted

Some words have been added to the lectionary text of the New Testament so that the faithful might be able to better under-stand and respond in faith to the scriptural proclamation. On the other hand, when the scriptures are read during the liturgy some phrases are dropped so as not to impede a faith-filled response to the proclamation of God's word.

Because they are harsh…on some occasions verses of scripture are omitted from the liturgical reading because of the apparent harshness of their language. Some years ago theologians might have described these verses as "offensive to pious ears," even if they formed part of our canonical scriptures. The Sunday congregation does not hear, for example, that anyone who joins himself to a prostitute becomes one body with her (1 Cor 6:16; 2nd Sunday of Year A) or that we Christians may be false witnesses to God (1 Cor 15:13-15; 6th Sunday of Year C).[128]

Along the same lines, the lectionary omits the passage which describes non-Jews as having handed themselves over to licentiousness and every kind of impurity to excess (Eph 4:18-19; 18th Sunday of Year B).[129] It does not encourage the members of the congregation to avoid all filth and evil excess (James 1:19-21a; 22nd Sunday of Year B). Similarly, when the scriptures are read to the congregation on Sunday, the lectionary text carefully avoids the lists of sins which provoke God's wrath, sins, that is, which had previously been characteristic of the lives of those to whom the word of God is presently addressed (Col 3:6-8; 18th Sunday of Year C).

*Because they don't fit in with the feast...*some verses are omitted from the proclamation of the scriptures so as to accommodate the scriptures to a particular feast or season that is being celebrated. Thus, Romans 5:3-4 is omitted from the Lenten reading on the third Sunday in Year A, 1 Corinthians 12:8-11 from the feast of Pentecost, Ephesians 1:7-18 from the second Sunday after Christmas, and Hebrews 5:1-6 from the Good Friday liturgy. By means of these omissions the assigned readings from the apostolic writings achieve greater thematic harmony with the feasts being celebrated. In each of the latter three instances, however, the omitted verses are read when the scriptures are being read in semi-continuous fashion. In the case of Romans, the omitted verses are read on Trinity Sunday in Year C.

*Or because the text has achieved autonomy in the liturgy...*on the twelfth Sunday of Year C, we listen to a reading from Paul's letter to the Galatians which includes the important baptismal formula, "There does not exist among you Jew or Greek, slave or freeman, male or female" (Gal 3:26-29).[130] When Paul wrote these words, they served to explain his affirmation that, because of faith, we are no longer under a disciplinarian, that is, the law. The letter clearly indicates that Paul is about to offer an explanation; Galatians 3:26 begins with an explanatory "for" (*gar*). Taken out of its epistolary context and adapted for liturgical use, Paul's explanation loses its explanatory character. The liturgical text of Galatians 3:26-28 has dropped the introductory "for" (*gar*).[131] The result is that Paul's words have become a catechesis on baptism. In the liturgy, they no longer serve to argue a theological point on the basis of the baptismal experience of the Christian communi-ty. They have become a reflection on baptism in and of itself. Unfortunately, and as has already been noted, the current lec-tionary's opening "in Christ Jesus" is misplaced. Rather than identifying the object of faith, this phrase describes our bap-tismal state as existence "in Christ Jesus."

In Year A, 1 Peter 2:20-25, appointed for liturgical reading on the fourth Sunday of the Easter season, begins with a rhetorical "but" (*alla*). The "but" links these verses to their scriptural con-text. The verses form part of a rhetorical argument urging slaves to obey their masters. Since the liturgical reading has been taken away from its biblical context, the telltale "but" has been removed. In effect, the rhetorical link of the passage to a context which deals with slavery has been "cosmetically" removed. On the sixth Sunday of Easter in Year A, the New Testament reading from 1 Peter 3:15-18 is part of a longer exhortation whose theme is bearing up under adversity. Its reference to Christ as Lord is presented as a contrast experience to fear and intimidation. The lectionary foregoes the contrast and with it the "but"[132] which serves as its textual marker in 1 Peter 3:15 in order to begin the liturgical reading on an upbeat note, the exhortation to "sanctify Christ as Lord in your hearts."

Chapter and Verse

In the thirteenth century, Stephen Langton, the archbishop of Canterbury, divided the New Testament into the chapters that we presently have. In the sixteenth century the several chapters were divided into verses. Since then the division of the biblical text into chapter and verse has become traditional. Roman Catholics continue to be amazed by how readily Christians of other faith traditions are able to identify the passages of scripture by chapter and verse when they themselves are not able to do so.

The medieval system of dividing the scriptures into chapter and verse serves a useful purpose. It enables us to easily identify a particular passage of scripture. Nevertheless, those who divided the New Testament into chapter and verse in this manner did not have the advantages available to modern biblical scholars. Nor were they always consistent in their division of the text. As a result, the reading of the New Testament according to the customary division often leaves many modern readers unsatisfied.

Biblical scholars might add that the traditional division into chapter and verse sometimes separates material that really belongs together. The lectionary text recognizes the somewhat arbitrary character of the traditional division when it appoints 1 Corinthians 11:1, 2 Corinthians 5:1, Ephesians 5:1-2, 1 Thessalonians 4:1-2, Hebrews 5:7-9 and James 4:1-3 to be read as the liturgical continuation of passages found in the preceding chapters of the New Testament. In similar fashion the lectionary requires that 1 Corinthians 12:31 be read as the introduction to 1 Corinthians 13 on the fourth Sunday of Year C.

The lectionary also recognizes the artificial character of the traditional division of the New Testament into chapter and verse when it assumes one half of the verse, but not the other, into the text that is appointed for liturgical reading. On the fourth Sunday of Easter (Year A), for example, the lectionary omits the rhetorical question of 1 Peter 2:20a, "What credit is there if you are patient when beaten for doing wrong?" On the twenty-second Sunday of the year (Year B) the lectionary includes the second part of James 1:21, "humbly welcome the word that has been planted in you and is able to save your souls," but not the first part, "put away all filth and evil excess."

Preachers who prepare their homilies, with the text of the New Testament rather than that of the lectionary at hand, should be aware that the lectionary's selection of passages for liturgical reading is on the basis of sense units rather than on the basis of the Bible's traditional chapter and verse. Consultation of the lectionary will help them to avoid overly focusing the homily on a scriptural passage which has not been read to the assembly. Nonetheless, it is good for preachers to read the liturgical selections in the bible itself so as to have an appreciation of the biblical context from which the liturgical readings have been taken.

10

Something's Been Left Out!

When the Christian assembly gathers for worship it does not listen to the reading of the entire New Testament, not even when it gathers over an extended period of time. Even when we understand "liturgy" in its most comprehensive sense, that is, the public worship of the church, including not only the Sunday celebration of the eucharist but also the celebration of weekday eucharist, the sacraments, and the liturgy of the hours, we recognize that it is impossible to read the entire text of the New Testament—let alone that of the Hebrew scriptures—when the church comes together for its liturgy. Only certain passages can be read. Various criteria for the selection of the biblical passages to be read in the celebration of the liturgy of the word have been identified in the introduction to the *Lectionary for Mass*.

Some passages have been chosen on the basis of the intrinsic importance of their subject matter or because of the previous usage made of them in our liturgical tradition. In addition, the introduction notes:

> Certain rather lengthy passages have been carefully abbreviated and appear in both long and short forms to meet different circumstances....On pastoral grounds, biblical texts that are truly difficult are not used in the readings for Sundays and solemnities. The difficulty may be objective, based on the serious literary, critical or exegetical problems the text raises, or the difficulty may lie in the faithful's power to grasp the meaning of some texts....[133]

> Many liturgies, including the Roman liturgy, have traditionally omitted certain verses from biblical readings....For

pastoral reasons, it seemed best to continue this tradition, taking care that the essential meaning of the text remain unchanged....[134]

A comparison of the lectionary text of the New Testament with the text of the New Testament itself enables us to identify those passages which the compilers of the lectionary considered to be "truly difficult" or not to be ranked among the "principal portions" of the scripture. Some awareness of what those passages are might be helpful as we read through Paul's letters and the other apostolic writings as part of our long-range preparation for preaching the epistles.

Romans

Omitted from Paul's letter to the Romans is the liturgical reading of Paul's long discussion on the sinfulness of Gentiles and Jews (Rom 1:18–3:20),[135] a text which includes the summary reflection on homosexuality and lesbianism (Rom 1:26-27), so problematic for many Christians today. Similarly missing from the lectionary is the long discussion about justification by faith apart from the works of the law (Rom 3:28–4:17). Nonetheless the lectionary has introduced the topic on the ninth Sunday of Year A (Rom 3:21-25, 28) and has followed up this introduction by presenting Abraham as an example of faith (Rom 4:18-25, 10th Sunday, Year A).

Another passage that has been omitted is Romans 6:12–8:8. This passage is another long discussion on sin. It includes the reference to the problematic "wretched I" of Romans 7. Similarly passed over is Paul's dense scriptural argumentation on the failure of Israel to observe the law (Rom 9:6–10:7).

Paul's exhortation to avoid the scandal given by the eating of unclean foods is omitted (Rom 14:10–15:3), as is the much longer discussion of this issue in 1 Corinthians 8–10. Finally, those who gather for Sunday worship hear neither Paul's reflections on why he preached where he did nor the long series of greetings with which Paul concludes his letter to the Romans (Rom

15:10–16:23). The reading of the many names of those to whom Paul sends his greetings might be tedious for the Community of Saint Mary Magdalene in Winter Park, but Paul's words provide valuable insights into how an early church was organized.

I have not attempted to cite each and every verse of Paul's letter to the Romans which does not appear in the Sunday lectionary. Rather, I have chosen to point out only some of the longer passages which do not appear in the Sunday lectionary, along with some of the themes to which the faithful are thereby not exposed. It should, however, be noted that some of the topics which Paul addresses in his letters are treated in more than one letter, albeit in somewhat different fashion. Moreover the church considers as particularly significant to its liturgical life not only the Sunday celebration of the eucharist but also the celebration of its major feasts. As a result, although the Sunday lectionary may omit the reading of Paul's treatment of one or another major theme according to the letter to the Romans, the church may well have seen fit to address that issue on some other occasion.

For example, there is no reading from Romans 10:14–11:12 in the Sunday eucharistic liturgy. This important passage includes a reflection on the preaching of the gospel (Rom 10:14-18), which is otherwise important in the church's liturgy—it is used on the feast of Andrew the apostle (November 30). Romans 12:3–13:7 also does not appear in the selection of readings for the Sunday liturgy. This section of the letter contains Paul's discussion on the charismatic nature of the church and his exhortation that Christians be subject to civil authority. A parallel, and fuller, Pauline exposition on the charismatic nature of the church, in 1 Corinthians 12, has, however, been appointed for reading on Pentecost Sunday.

1 Corinthians

Although readings from 1 Corinthians occur in each year of the three year liturgical cycle,[136] some portions of this letter are not read to the faithful when they gather for Sunday worship.

Food Offered to Idols

By the time that someone reading Paul's first letter to the Corinthians comes to the matter of food offered to idols (1 Corinthians 8), he or she is well aware that one of the apostle's favorite argumentative techniques is for him to begin the exposition of the matter at hand, digress for a while, and then return to the principal point of the exposition. A-B-A' is the classic way of schematizing this rhetorical pattern. When Paul uses this kind of rhetoric in 1 Corinthians, his aside (element B in the schema) often touches upon a matter of principle which clarifies the expository material. It serves as a kind of exemplary argument.

Paul's technique of argument by digression is effectively used in 1 Corinthians 12–14. Expressing a concern that some members of the community have been unduly attracted to ecstatic phenomena, Paul digresses from the matter at hand to reflect with the Corinthians on love which is the greatest of all the spiritual gifts (1 Corinthians 13). Love, the gift of the Holy Spirit, he explains in his digression, is the ground of all the charisms. In this instance, both the clarifying aside of 1 Corinthians 13 and the enveloping context of Paul's dealing with a community's fascination with spiritual gifts are found in our Sunday liturgy, namely, on the second, third, and fourth Sundays of Year C.

An argument by digression also occurs in 1 Corinthians 8–10. Paul writes about his willingness to forego his apostolic rights (1 Corinthians 9) while arguing that the Corinthians should be attentive to the situation of the weak who are scandalized by the eating of food offered to idols. Paul's willingness to forego even his apostolic rights should serve as an example to those who consider themselves strong and willing to give up something for the benefit of the weak. This intervenient passage (1 Corinthians 9) is represented in the Sunday liturgy by a small snippet which treats of Paul's reward for preaching the gospel (1 Cor 9:16-19, 22-23; 5th Sunday, Year B), but the lectionary omits any mention of the longer section which deals with food offered to idols (1 Cor 8–10).

The reason is simple. The matter of food offered to idols is not one which is of immediate concern to the majority of Christians today. Nonetheless, I personally recall, and very vividly, my experience with a young Japanese woman, about to be received into the Catholic Church, who continued to place the first glass of water drawn from the tap each day in front of the small statue of Buddha which she maintained in her home. While the issue which Paul addresses in 1 Corinthians 8–10 might seem to be pertinent in non-Western cultures, it should not be forgotten that the larger issues which Paul considers in this passage are matters of considerable concern for Christians today. These larger issues are the extent and limits of freedom, inculturation and the integration of religious traditions, and the attitude of Christians vis-à-vis those of delicate conscience within the community.[137] These issues are germane to the Christian consideration of those who, for example, participate in witches' covens, but nevertheless continue regularly to come to church.

Gender and Sexuality

If pastoral considerations have apparently led to the omission of those passages dealing with food offered to idols from the lectionary, another body of pastoral reasons seems to have led to the lectionary's silence with regard to those passages in which Paul treats of the role of women in the church in a way which is so problematic for many Christian women today, namely, the tradition that women should pray with their heads veiled (1 Cor 11:2-16) and the contention that they should be silent in the churches (1 Cor 14:33-36).[138] Similarly avoided from the Sunday liturgical reading of 1 Corinthians is much of Paul's long disquisition on sexuality (1 Corinthians 5–7), including his admonitions on divorce (1 Cor 7:10-16).

The series of readings appointed for the Sundays in ordinary time in Year B begins with a short reflection on the body as the temple of the Holy Spirit (1 Cor 6:13-15, 17-20). On the following Sundays the readings first speak about the ephemeral nature of the present order (1 Cor 7:29-31) and then extol the spiritual advantages accruing to those who are unmarried (1 Cor 7:32-35).

At this point in the church's history, those who work in the family life ministry in St. Joseph's in Cupertino may regret the lectionary's omission of the reading of 1 Corinthians 7:10-16. The omission has deprived those who preach of a ready-made opportunity to address the congregation on the tradition of the church relative to divorce. On the other hand, many a preacher has breathed a sigh of relief because the congregation has not heard that reading from 1 Corinthians which deals with the exhortation to women to be veiled when they come into the assembly, and Paul's convoluted—at least to modern ears—reasoning as to why this peculiar pastoral practice should be followed (1 Cor 11:2-16).

Paul and Those Whom He Knew

One of the difficulties encountered by interpreters of 1 Corinthians is trying to ascertain the nature of the relationship between Paul and Apollos. The problem may have been the relationship between these two apostles or it may have been their relationship, as perceived and/or distorted by some of the Christians at Corinth. Our lectionary does not offer a reading from those extensive portions of the letter which deal with this issue, nor does it deal with Paul's apostolic sufferings (1 Corinthians 3–4) or speaking in tongues (1 Corinthians 14). A homily on speaking in tongues would certainly be appropriate in a world where glossolalia and other ecstatic phenomena are highly valued religious experiences.

1 Corinthians 16 is also absent from the lectionary. Thus the Sunday readings do not rehearse Paul's exhortation on the collection for the saints (1 Cor 16:1-4), even though a related passage, 2 Cor 8:7, 9, 13-15, is used on the thirteenth Sunday in ordinary time (Year B). Thus, too, there is omitted the series of final admonitions and greetings with which Paul brought his letter to closure. This omission means that the faithful are not exposed to one of the more blatantly epistolary features of Paul's letter. That Paul typically concludes his letters with a series of short directives and extends his greetings to various people serves as a striking indication that he has written texts which are really letters. The finale of 1 Corinthians is not the only epistolary conclusion that does not appear in the Sunday lectionary. The lec-

tionary omits from its selection of Sunday lections the final admonitions and greetings of many of Paul's authentic letters.

To be sure, the staccato pace of the final directives and the fact that those whom Paul greets are, for the most part, persons whose names may not even be recognized by the typical Sunday congregation implies that it might be difficult for a congregation adequately to grasp the meaning of these final passages in Paul's letters. On the other hand, the names found at the end of 1 Corinthians—Timothy, Apollos, Stephanas, Fortunatus, Achaicus, Aquila, and Prisca—are well enough known to warrant some mention from the pulpit. In any event, the pastoral decision not to include Paul's farewell greetings in the lectionary means that something has been lost. This something is the awareness that Paul was writing real letters to real people, in their flesh-and-blood and day-to-day experience.

There are, of course, exceptions in this regard. Some of the lectionary's selections from Paul's letters show full well that he had written real letters to real people. Particularly striking is the lectionary's choice of readings from the shorter letters in which Paul's involvement with the community to which he is writing is more than obvious. These more personal letters, those to the Thessalonians, Galatians, and Philippians, are well represented in the cycle of liturgical readings for Sundays and major feasts. Because these are letters in which Paul has clearly invested himself in a very personal and engaging fashion, it is fitting that they should be well-represented in the cycle of liturgical readings.

1 Thessalonians, Galatians, Philippians

1 Thessalonians is the oldest of Paul's authentic letters. It was written some twenty years after Jesus died and about fifteen years after Paul had first confessed Jesus as Lord. The opening greetings of this letter as well as some of its final admonitions are read to the faithful when the text is read on the last few Sundays of ordinary time (29th, 32nd and 33rd Sundays, Year A).

Absent from the lectionary's reading of 1 Thessalonians is Paul's personal reflection on the visit which he had made to the community shortly before he wrote his letter (1 Thess 2:1-6). The lectionary also omits Paul's expression of ongoing concern for the community and the measures which he had taken in order to assuage his own anxiety in its regard (1 Thess 3:1-11). Notably absent as well is the proclamation of Paul's exhortation on sexual morality and Christian charity (1 Thess 4:3-12).[139]

Before the congregation listens to the reading of passages from the oldest of Paul's letters, it has heard selections from his letter to the Philippians. This letter may well be the most personal of all the letters. Passages from its final chapter are read on the twenty-seventh and twenty-eighth Sundays in ordinary time (Year A), but the lectionary avoids Paul's grateful reminiscence of the Philippians with which the letter begins. The omitted passage (Phil 1:3-11) is a marvelous expression of ministerial thanksgiving, one which can well serve to inspire all who are engaged in the work of evangelization.

Apart from that singular omission, what the lectionary omits from its reading of Paul's letter to the Philippians are the kinds of things that are omitted from 1 Thessalonians and the letter to the Galatians, that is, the autobiographical material (Phil 1:12-19; 2:12-30; 3:9-16) and the harsh expressions of Philippians 3:1-2.

Paul's letter to the Galatians is a very personal letter, but the nature of his relationship with the Galatians is quite different from the kind of relationship that he had with Christians in Thessalonica and Philippi. The churches of Galatia were evangelized by Paul, but their subsequent way of life was one which the apostle found difficult to accept. Passages from Galatians are read in semi-continuous fashion immediately after the series of readings from 1 Corinthians on the Sundays of ordinary time in Year C. The letter opens with a thinly veiled defense of Paul's apostolate and a strong admonition. It closes with a reflection on what really matters and the letter's final salutation. Both the opening and closing of this letter occur in the series of Sunday readings (9th-14th Sundays, Year C). Although Paul's apostolic authority is a major issue at stake in the letter to the Galatians, the lectionary omits from its semi-continuous reading the tale of Paul's extensive and heartfelt reflection on his apostolate (Gal

1:11–2:14)—passages which are, nonetheless, appointed for weekday reading.[140]

Galatians is perhaps the most passionate of Paul's letters. Many of those passages in which Paul displays his emotion—sometimes his unmeasured emotion—have been omitted from the liturgical selection. Paul's midrashic reflections on the story of Abraham also do not come up for Sunday reading (Gal 3:1-25; 4:8–5:12). Another surprising omission is that of Paul's contrast between the works of the flesh and the fruits of the Spirit (5:19-23). The latter omission is particularly striking; the passage is used so often in the church's catechesis.[141]

2 Corinthians and Philemon

2 Corinthians is one of the longest letters in the Pauline corpus—and for that reason it occupies the third position in the canonical collection of the apostle's correspondence. As has been noted, an increasing number of biblical scholars consider that this letter was not originally composed by Paul as a single letter. They think that Paul's so-called second letter to the Corinthians represents a collection of fragments of various letters which Paul had written to the Corinthians. According to the theory, the fragments would have been gathered together and put into the form of a single letter by one of Paul's disciples sometime after the apostle's death.

Whether the so-called second letter to the Corinthians is a collection of epistolary fragments or not, the lectionary treats 2 Corinthians in very fragmental fashion. The letter is not substantially represented among the lections appointed for the celebration of the eucharist on Sundays. A series of four readings in Year B incorporates some of Paul's reflections on ministry and mortality—especially insofar as Jesus is thereby manifest (2 Cor 4:6–5:17)—but otherwise the second letter to the Corinthians is only intermittently reflected in the Sunday lections. Since 2 Corinthians is arguably one of the more enigmatic of Paul's letters, the relatively sparse use made of it in the liturgy reflects a truly balanced pastoral judgment as to the usefulness of reading the letter to an assembly which gathers for the celebration of the eucharist on Sunday.

Philemon and the Church in His House

Had 2 Corinthians been written as a single composition, it would have been one of Paul's longer letters. In contrast, the letter to Philemon and the church in his house[142] is the shortest of Paul's extant letters. It deals with the slave Onesimus who had sought the apostle's support and who was preparing to return to his master.[143] The letter is one of commendation, in which Paul asks Philemon to treat Onesimus as his [Paul's] very own son.

The topicality of Paul's personal appeal makes the letter to Philemon somewhat irrelevant to contemporary Christian congregations. Similarly, Paul's reflection on slavery in 1 Corinthians 7:21-24 is omitted from the Sunday lectionary, as are those passages in Ephesians and Colossians which deal with the topic (Eph 6:5-9; Col 3:22-4:1). The letter to Philemon is, nonetheless, part of the church's scriptural heritage, and so it has been included in the Sunday lectionary. The snippet chosen as a scriptural reading begins with an appeal from Paul, now in his declining years, to Philemon "on the basis of love" (Phlm 9-10, 12-17; 23rd Sunday, Year C).

Other Pauline Epistles

Ephesians, Colossians, 2 Thessalonians, 1 and 2 Timothy, and Titus belong to the Pauline tradition and have been inspired by the living memory of the apostle ministering to churches which he had evangelized. They reflect the effort of those churches to embody anew the living tradition of the apostle. Although biblical scholars today are increasingly convinced that these texts have not been written by the apostle, they remain apostolic writings.[144] Nonetheless, significant portions of these epistles do not appear in our lectionary.

Ephesians, Colossians, and 2 Thessalonians

Of these six epistles, the one to the Ephesians is best represented in the Sunday lectionary. The lectionary does not, however, include its imaginative passage on the relationship between the ascended Christ and his church which speaks about the charismatic nature of the universal church (Eph 4:7-16). Nor does it include the epistle's conventional exhortation to avoid untruth, fornication, and improper speech (Eph 4:25-29) or the admonitions with which the epistle closes (Eph 6).

As a first draft of the epistle to the Ephesians, the epistle to the Colossians is not as well represented in the Sunday lectionary as is Ephesians. The lectionary avoids a reading of that portion of Colossians which plays with the theme of the body—Paul's, Christ's, and the Christian's (Col 2:1-11). The pericope which deals with strange cultic observances (Col 2:15-23)—an unfortunate omission for those who must deal with the New Age cult in our times!—the staccato paraenesis of Colossians 3:5-11, and the final chapter (Colossians 4) with its various admonitions and literary greetings are also omitted from the lectionary.

As the epistle to the Ephesians is a new and revised edition of Colossians, the second epistle to the Thessalonians is a radical revision of Paul's letter to the Thessalonians. The heart of the new text is its revision of Paul's apocalyptic scenario, so dear to many preachers of the fundamentalist ilk. It is, however, precisely this section which is not taken up in the Sunday lectionary (2 Thess 2:3-12; cf. 2 Thess 1:4-10).[145]

The Pastoral Epistles

The first letter of Paul to Timothy is essentially a document on church order, with extensive directives with regard to bishops, presbyters, deacons, and widows. The sections dealing with these ministries comprise the heart of the text. It is, however, precisely these passages, including the entirety of 1 Timothy 2:9–6:10, which are omitted from the Sunday lectionary. As one might expect, the lectionary carefully avoids the exhortation that women should be silent in the churches (1 Tim 2:11-15). It also passes over in silence a general moral exhortation which cites the Lord Jesus Christ as an example (1 Tim 6:11-16).

While 2 Timothy is generally well represented in the Sunday lectionary, its readings do not include the long exhortation to avoid various patterns of anti-social behavior (2 Tim 2:14–3:13) and the "biographical fragments" (2 Tim 4:9-15, 19-21). These bio-bits serve to provide the epistle with some verisimilitude and contribute to its character as a farewell document, akin to the farewell discourses of the biblical tradition.

The epistle to Titus' directives on church order, like those of 1 Timothy, are not recited in the Sunday liturgy. This means that the substance of this apostolic writing is not offered to the faithful. On the other hand, the Christmas liturgy does make use of two passages that speak of the appearance, literally, the "epiphany," of Jesus Christ our savior (Tit 2:11-14; 3:4-7). Together these two readings from Titus appear as a single lection for the solemnity of the Baptism of the Lord, in Year C in the New Order of Readings.

The "Letter to the Hebrews"

In the canon of the New Testament, the so-called letter to the Hebrews is clearly an appendage to the Pauline corpus. One of its unique features is that it includes extensive reflection on the Jewish scriptures. To a large extent this reflection has been omitted from the Sunday lectionary's selection of passages from Hebrews. The lectionary passes over in silence Hebrews 1:7–2:8 and 2:12–4:11, thereby omitting a very significant reflection on the humanity of Jesus, one which is perhaps the New Testament's most profound and systematic discussion of what it means for Jesus to have been human. In the light of the present pastoral situation of the church in the United States, when there is so much discussion about the historical Jesus, this is a regrettable omission. The inclusion of Hebrews 2:5-18 in the lectionary would have provided a homilist with a good opportunity to preach about the significance of the humanity of Jesus.

The Sunday lectionary also omits a long reflection on

Abraham (Heb 5:11–7:22). The first eucharistic prayer proclaims Abraham as our father in faith, but to a large extent Abraham remains a great mystery for many churchgoers today. How well I remember the priest who, upon reading about Abraham in some hints for homilists published by one of the homiletic services, asked me, "What has Abraham got to do with our faith?" This priest had been celebrating mass according to the Latin text of the Roman rite for almost forty years, but failed to appreciate the significance of Abraham. The new edition of the order of readings has somewhat compensated for this lacuna by presenting Abraham and Sarah—a noteworthy inclusion!—along with Isaac, as persons of faith in the reading now appointed for the solemnity of the Holy Family (Year B).[146]

Similarly absent from the lectionary's selection of readings from Hebrews is the disquisition on Moses, the sanctuary and the covenant (Heb 7:29–9:10), and that on the sanctuary and its sacrifices (Heb 10:1-10, 19-39), along with the disparate moral paraenesis of the exhortation's final chapter (Hebrews 13).

The Catholic Epistles

Taking the Catholic epistles, as they appear in their canonical order, we begin with the epistle of James. Absent from the lectionary is the epistle's important reflection on the relationship among love, freedom, and the decalogue (James 2:8-13). The lectionary rehearses James' exposition on faith and works, a counterpoint to Paul's teaching on faith and works,[147] but fails to add the companion piece, which cites Abraham and Rahab[148] as biblical examples of the importance of works (James 2:19-26). James' moral exhortation to guard one's tongue is likewise omitted (James 3:1-12), as is the reflection on the various causes of strife (James 4:3-12).

The most striking of the Sunday lectionary's omission of passages from James must be, however, that of the epistle's material on prayer for the sick, including James 5:14, the verse which the Council of Trent (1551) had cited as the scriptural warrant for the sacrament of anointing.[149]

The Petrine and Johannine Epistles

Although the first epistle of Peter is well represented in the liturgical lections appointed for Sundays, the text's traditional catechesis on a suitable attitude toward civil authority and the attitudes appropriate to domestic conduct (1 Pet 2:13–20; 3:1-7) has been omitted.[150] The lectionary's omission of 1 Peter's exhortations on civil authority and slavery parallels the lectionary's omission of similar material in the Pauline corpus. The lectionary likewise generally overlooks the final chapters of this epistle, including its important address to elders and the faithful (1 Pet 5:1-5).

The second letter of Peter has not been assumed into the semi-continuous reading of texts appointed for ordinary time; thus its synopsis of primal history, to a large extent based on the epistle of Jude, does not appear in the Sunday lectionary. Neither does the Sunday lectionary make use of the epistle of Jude.

The second and third epistles of John appear to be real letters, but they do not appear in our Sunday lectionary. On the other hand, the first letter of John is of some importance in that the lectionary has a selection of six semi-continuous readings appointed for reading in the Easter season of Year B.

Epilogue

The lectionary's selection of passages to be read on Sundays and feast days is substantial, but it is not as extensive as is the selection of readings for the weekday celebration of the eucharist. When a homilist reviews the selection of passages from Paul's letters and the apostolic writings which have been appointed for Sunday reading, he or she is probably surprised to learn that more than one memorable passage has been omitted. On the other hand the same homilist is most likely quite relieved to learn that the lectionary has taken care to remove from the roster of texts assigned for public reading some of the more problematic passages of the epistles.

What remains is, nonetheless, a fitting echo of the gospel

according to Paul. This version of the gospel is one that needs to be preached. The apostle has taught us that there is but one gospel of Christ (Gal 1:7). The many echoes of this single proclamation must be heard, so that the entire church might more faithfully confess that Jesus is Lord.[151]

Notes

1. See especially *Paul and the Thessalonians: The Philosophic Tradition of Pastoral Care* (Philadelphia: Fortress, 1987).

2. November 21, 1964.

3. November 18, 1965.

4. See also the first paragraph of the introduction to the *Lectionary for Mass* which cites this very paragraph of *Dei Verbum*, as does the Pontifical Biblical Commission's "The Interpretation of the Bible in the Church," IV, C, 1 (*Origins*, 23 [1994] 497-524, p. 522).

5. *General Instruction of the Roman Missal*, 34.

6. *Dei Verbum*, 21.

7. *Dei Verbum*, 25. Cf. Jerome, *Commentary on Isaiah*, Prologue (PL 24, 17). This passage from the prologue of Jerome's commentary on Isaiah has been incorporated into the office of readings for the feast of St. Jerome (September 30). It has also been cited in two of this century's most important papal encyclicals on the study of the bible, Benedict XV's *Spiritus Paraclitus* (1920) and Pius XII's *Divino Afflante Spiritu* (1943).

8. Roman Missal, 33. Cf. "Interpretation of the Bible," IV, C, 1.

9. "Interpretation of the Bible," IV, C, 1.

10. "Interpretation of the Bible," IV, C, 1. The quotation is from *Sacrosanctum Concilium*, 7. Cf. *General Instruction of the Roman Missal*, 33.

11. See the introduction to the *Lectionary for Mass*, par. 8.

12. See *Comme le prévoit*, par. 31, in International Commission on English in the Liturgy, *Documents on the Liturgy 1963-1979: Conciliar, Papal and Curial Texts* (Collegeville, MN: The Liturgical Press, 1982) 288.

13. See the introduction to the *New Order of Readings*, par. 61.

14. Cf. "Interpretation of the Bible," IV, C, 1, 3.

15. See Josef A. Jungmann, *The Mass: An Historical, Theological, and Pastoral Survey* (Collegeville, MN: Liturgical, 1976) 180.

16. Cf. "Interpretation of the Bible," IV, C, 1.

17. Cf. "Interpretation of the Bible," IV, C, 1.

18. Cf. Luke 4:16-30.

19. *Sacrosanctum concilium*, 52.

20. See J.A. Jungmann, *The Mass*, 180.

21. Paragraphs 24 and 52 of the constitution mentions the "homily" (*homilia*; cf. pars. 53, 78), but this paragraph (No. 35), more legislative in its tone, speaks of the "sermon" (*sermo*).

22. See "Interpretation of the Bible," IV, C, 3.

23. The ancient patristic image of the table of the word of God and of the body of Christ is taken up again in *Dei Verbum*, 21, and the *General Instruction of the Roman Missal*, 8. Having affirmed that the two parts of the eucharistic liturgy are so closely connected as to form but one act of worship, it identifies the table of God's word with the reading of the scriptures (Par. 34) and the table of Christ's body with the altar (Par. 49).

24. Introduction to the *New Order of Readings*, par. 38.

25. *General Instruction of the Roman Missal*, par. 41.

26. In his April 3, 1969 apostolic constitution *Missale Romanum*, Paul VI spoke of the faithful's "hunger for the word of God." See *Documents on the Liturgy* 1963-1979, 460.

27. See introduction to the *New Order of Readings*, par. 45.

28. Whether the feeding of God's people is something that only "pastors" can do is another issue. The issue is one which lies beyond the purview of the present volume, whose principal purpose is to reflect on the possibility of preaching from the epistles during the celebration of the Sunday eucharist. What it has to say will hopefully prove to be helpful to those who conduct eucharistic services on Sunday in so-called priestless parishes. Hopefully, too, it may be of service to those laity who preach on occasions other than that of the celebration of eucharist.

29. See *Lumen Gentium*, 25.

30. See Simon Tugwell, *The Way of the Preacher* (Springfield, IL: Templegate, 1979) 23.

31. See *Lumen Gentium*, 28.

32. See the introduction to the *New Order of Readings*, par. 63,

33. In this regard a similar situation exists in Protestant congregations as well as in Catholic parishes. With regard to the Protestant experience, see Robert Jewett, *Paul: The Apostle to America* (Louisville: Westminster/John Knox, 1994) 14-18.

34. See the introduction to the *New Order of Readings*, 18.

35. See also John F. O'Grady, *Pillars of Paul's Gospel: Galatians and Romans* (New York-Mahwah: Paulist, 1992) 167.

36. See my *Letters That Paul Did Not Write: The Epistle to the Hebrews and the Pauline Pseudepigrapha*. Good News Studies, 28 (Wilmington, DE: Glazier, 1988) 88-208.

37. Cf. Joseph A. Fitzmyer, *Romans: A New Translation with*

Introduction and Commentary (Anchor Bible 33. Garden City, NY: Doubleday, 1993); Jean-Noël Aletti, *Saint Paul: Epître aux Colossiens* (Etudes bibliques. Paris: Gabalda, 1993).

38. This is not the place to enter into a scholarly discussion of the probable dependence of Ephesians on Colossians and of 2 Peter 2 on Jude. See my *Letters That Paul Did Not Write*, 143-144; John H. Elliott,"Peter, Second Epistle of," *ABD*, 5, 282-287, esp. 284; Victor P. Furnish,"Ephesians, Epistle to the," *ABD*, 2, 535-542, esp. 536-537.

39. See Myles M. Bourke, "The Epistle to the Hebrews," *New Jerome Biblical Commentary*, 921.

40. See 1 Thess 5:27.

41. The rendering of the New American Bible, still used in most lectionaries in the United States at the present time, was "Paul, Silvanus and Timothy to the church of Thessalonians who belong to God the Father and the Lord Jesus Christ." With regard to the translation"who belong to" (as a translation of the simple preposition"*en*-in"), the NAB is overly specific, but its version provides a marvelous basis for a reflection on what it means to belong to a local congregation of believers.

42. See the *General Instruction of the Roman Missal*, which notes that"the homily…should develop some point of the readings or of another text from the Ordinary or the Mass of the day" (Par. 42).

43. In this regard, see the various articles written in recent years by Mary Catherine Hilkert of the Order of Preachers.

44. Paul refers to the "collection for the holy ones" (1 Cor 16:1) in Rom 15:26-27; 1 Cor 16:1-4; 2 Cor 8–9; Gal 2:10. In regard to the collection, see especially Jouette M. Bassler, *God and Mammon: Asking for Money in the New Testament* (Nashville, TN: Abingdon, 1991).

45. The fact that the author of Colossians is not so engaged serves as an argument against its Pauline authorship. See Mark Kiley,

Colossians as Pseudepigraphy (The Biblical Seminar. Sheffield: JSOT Press, 1986) 46-51, 108-118, 126-127.

46. Par. 63.

47. See my *Letters That Paul Did Not Write*.

48. Technically these six texts can be called the deutero-Pauline writings or the Pauline pseudepigrapha. Calling them "deutero-Pauline" indicates that they were more recently attributed to Paul. Calling them "Pauline pseudepigrapha" indicates that they were incorrectly attributed to Paul.

49. See, for example, their respective household codes (Col 3:18-4:1; Eph 5:21–6:9).

50. Other lectionaries of that time, for example, the approved Dutch-language lectionary (1970), used the simple introduction on Christmas and on Good Friday.

51. See the introduction to the *New Order of Readings*, par. 122e. The introduction identifies this presentation of the title of Hebrews as a specific exception to the general principle that "the traditionally accepted titles for books are to be retained." One might also note that during the Christmas season the liturgy of the hours introduces the scriptural readings as "From the letter to the Colossians," whereas it uses "From the second letter of the apostle Paul to the Corinthians" as the introductory formula when this letter is read during ordinary time.

52. In his 1943 encyclical, *Divino Afflante Spiritu*, the magna charta of modern Catholic biblical scholarship, Pius XII, while recognizing that the accommodated use of scripture is occasionally useful in preaching, called the practice "extrinsic and adventitious to holy scripture" and said that it "is not without its dangers, especially today."

53. See also the introduction to the *New Order of Readings*, especially par. 39: "The first requirement for one who is to preside over the celebration is a thorough knowledge of the structure of the

order of readings so that he will know how to inspire good effects in the hearts of the faithful. Through study and prayer he must also develop a full understanding of the coordination and connection of the various texts in the liturgy of the word, so that the order of readings will become the source of a sound understanding of the mystery of Christ and his saving work."

54. Introduction to the Lectionary, par. 8b.

55. See the introduction to the Lectionary, par. 8e.

56. See the *General Instruction of the Roman Missal*, par. 319.

57. To enhance the appreciation of the semi-continuous reading of the biblical texts, the introduction to the *New Order of Readings* suggests that the Sunday lectionary be divided into a three-year cycle"so that all the readings for each year are presented in sequence." See introduction to the *New Order of Readings*, par. 113.

58. See Ernest Best, *From Text to Sermon: Responsible Use of the New Testament in Preaching* (Atlanta: John Knox, 1978) 65-75.

59. See Walter Vogels, *Reading & Preaching the Bible: A New Semiotic Approach* (Background Books 4. Wilmington, DE: Glazier, 1986) 17-21.

60. The New Revised Standard Version was approved for liturgical usage by both the Canadian Conference of Catholic Bishops and the National Conference of Catholic Bishops in the United States during the fall of 1991. Their decisions were approved by the Vatican's Congregation of Divine Worship and the Discipline of the Sacraments. On October 25, 1994, Archbishop Geraldo Agnelo announced that the approval had been withdrawn. It was suggested that officials of the Congregation for the Doctrine of the Faith had found fault with its use of inclusive language. On November 9 officials of the Canadian Conference of Catholic Bishops announced that discussions with the Vatican would continue with regard to particular points of the NRSV translation. Representatives of the (U.S.) National Conference of Catholic

Bishops met with Vatican officials on January 19 and 20, 1995. In the meantime the Canadian lectionary, based on the NRSV, continues to be used throughout Canada.

61. I hold that 2 John and 3 John were genuine letters. Their author simply identifies himself as "the elder." In any event, these letters are not used in the Sunday lectionary. The epistle of Jude is not really a letter nor is the epistle to the Hebrews. Because the latter so clearly has the form of a discourse, it is preferable to refer to it as a homily, a discourse, a reflection, rather than as a letter or an epistle.

62. See A.J.M. Wedderburn, "Keeping Up with Recent Studies: Some Recent Pauline Chronologies," *Expository Times* 92 (1981) 103-108. In the *New Jerome Biblical Commentary*, Joseph A. Fitzmyer and Raymond E. Brown offer 1 Thessalonians, Galatians, Philippians, Philemon, 1 Corinthians, 2 Corinthians, Romans as the relative sequence of Paul's letters (NJBC [Englewood Cliffs, NJ: Prentice Hall, 1990] 779-780 and 1045).

63. See, however, Rom 16:21-23.

64. This is the so-called "lost letter" to the Corinthians. It is, in any case, no longer extant. Some scholars, however, believe that Paul did not write very long letters to the Corinthians. They opine that Paul wrote several shorter letters to the Corinthians and that a later editor combined these shorter texts into two longer texts, the canonical 1 and 2 Corinthians. If this were the case, the "lost letter" would have been largely incorporated into the two canonical letters of Paul to the Corinthians.

65. Suetonius, *Life of Claudius*, 25, 4. Acts 18:2 indicates that some Jewish Christians left Rome because of this edict, generally believed to have been decreed in 49 A.D.

66. On these topics, see David P. Efroymson, et al., eds., *Within Context: Essays on Jews and Judaism in the New Testament* (Collegeville, MN: Liturgical, 1993).

67. For an overview of the current discussion, see Jerome Murphy-O'Connor, "The Second Letter to the Corinthians," *New Jerome Biblical Commentary*, 816-829, and Hans Dieter Betz, "Corinthians, Second Epistle to the," *Anchor Bible Dictionary*, 1, 1148-1154. Betz identifies six letter fragments, viz., a first apology (2 Cor 2:14–6:13; 7:2-4); a second apology (2 Cor 10:1–13:10); a letter of reconciliation (1:1–2:13; 7:5-16; 13:11-13); the administrative letter of chapter 8; the administrative letter of chapter 9; and the interpolation of 2 Cor 6:14–7:1. As is common in the discussion of the sources of biblical texts, scholars are generally agreed that our extant 2 Corinthians is compiled from earlier Pauline texts, but they do not agree among themselves on the details of the discernment and reconstruction of these sources.

68. Read on the seventh Sunday of the year, this passage occupies first place in the sequence of liturgical readings from the second letter to the Corinthians.

69. See, for example, Frank J. Matera, *Galatians* (Sacra Pagina 9. Collegeville, MN: Liturgical, 1992) 97-102. Technically, the issue is whether in the expression *pistis Iēsou Christou*, the genitive *Iēsou Christou* is an objective genitive (the traditional interpretation) or a subjective genitive (the more recent interpretation). We have a similar problem in interpreting the phrase, "the love of God": does this phrase mean our love for God (with God as the object of love) or does it mean God's love for us (with God as the subject of love)? The English translation of Paul's Greek requires the use of a different pronoun to render the different grammatical uses of the genitive; his context does not provide commentators with an easy answer as to how Paul has used the genitive.

70. See, for example, my article, "The Image of Paul in the Pastorals," *Laval théologique et philosophique* 31 (1975) 147-173, esp. 165-169.

71. William Dalton's introduction to 1 Peter in the *New Jerome Biblical Commentary* takes a position which is at odds with the trend of much modern biblical scholarship. Dalton suggests that the epistle comes from Peter, whose secretary Silvanus (1 Pet 5:12)

enjoyed considerable freedom in the composition of the text (see NJBC, 903).

72. Cf. Rev 1:4.

73. That the material was put together in the form of a letter is a tribute to the influence of Paul's apostolic letters on early Christian tradition. See, in this regard, my book, *The Birth of the New Testament: The Origin and Development of the First Christian Generation* (New York: Crossroad, 1993) 184-213.

74. These two instances are, in fact, the only instances in which the Sunday lectionary's choice of lections for semi-continuous reading does not follow the sequence in which the passages occur in the biblical text themselves.

75. See Richard P. McBrien, "The Future of the Church: Looking Toward the Third Christian Millennium," *Warren Lecture Series in Catholic Studies*, 14 (Tulsa, OK: University of Tulsa, 1991) 6. The problem of biblical fundamentalism is not limited to the United States. Some years ago I gave a series of lectures throughout Nigeria. On each occasion, I was asked a question about fundamentalism in the local churches. See also *International Papers in Pastoral Ministry* 3:4 (December 1992) 4.

76. A good indication of the state of things was the fact that, in 1990, the relatively new TPI series of commentaries chose to reprint John Sweet's 1979 Pelican commentary with but few modifications. Among the more recent works on Revelation, a homilist might consult with profit Richard Bauckham's *The Theology of the Book of Revelation* (New Testament Theology. Cambridge/New York: Cambridge University Press, 1993), Wilfrid Harrington's *Revelation* (Sacra Pagina 18. Collegeville, MN: Liturgical, 1993), and Charles H. Talbert's *The Apocalypse: A Reading of the Revelation of John* (Louisville: Westminster/John Knox, 1994).

77. In Year II, readings from the book of Revelation are assigned for the last two weeks in ordinary time.

78. The reading of 1 Thess 4:13-18 on the thirty-second Sunday of the year (Year A) presents another such opportunity. This reading is, however, a one-time occurrence. Pastorally, it does not present the advantages that accrue from a reading of apocalyptic literature on six successive Sundays.

One might also note that the reading of 1 Thess 4:13-18 may, for pastoral reasons, be shortened to 1 Thess 4:13-14. The reason for this pastoral option is the difficulty of understanding the apocalyptic portion of the reading. Ironically, it is precisely this difficulty which constitutes a major pastoral problem at the present time.

79. See Isa 64:3. The NRSV renders 1 Cor 2:9 as "What eye has not seen, and ear has not heard, and what has not entered the human heart, what God has prepared for those who love him."

80. See the Introduction to the *New Order of Readings*, par. 68.

81. The readings from the apostolic writings for the vigil mass of Christmas and for the feast of the Baptism of the Lord have been taken from the Acts of the Apostles, respectively 13:16-17, 22-25 and 10:34-38.

82. The introduction to the *New Order of Readings* states that the Old Testament reading and the gospel continue the Roman tradition; the text for the reading from the apostolic letters is about the calling of all peoples to salvation. See the introduction to the *New Order of Readings*, par. 95.

83. Those who moralize consistently tend to forget that much of the content of recent Roman Catholic moral reflection is the result of a philosophical analysis of human conduct. It is not immediately dependent upon our experience in faith.

84. "Interpretation of the Bible," IV, C, 3.

85. Ibid.

86. It is interesting to note that, whereas the Sunday liturgy rehearses the maternal image used by Paul to describe his relationship with the Thessalonians (1 Thess 2:7) on the thirty-first

Sunday of Year A, it does not reiterate Paul's use of the paternal image in 1 Thess 2:11.

87. Cf. Matt 22:35-40; Luke 10:25-28. The Markan text is used as a gospel reading on thirtieth Sunday of Year A. The unity of the twofold commandment of love is most clearly expressed in the Lukan version where a single use of the verb "love" has a double object, namely, God and neighbor (Luke 10:27). In the Lukan version of the scene, Jesus, as a good teacher, follows the Socratic method in eliciting this basic insight from the scholar of the law.

88. See the similar list of qualities for a deacon in 1 Tim 3:8-12 and for a bishop in Titus 1:7-9. The discerning reader should not, however, too readily identify the office of bishop in today's church with the office of "bishop" to which the pastoral epistles refer. Hence, in a footnote the New Revised Standard Version suggests that a better translation might be "overseer." The text is generally addressing itself to the function of oversight in the church. See my "Pastoral Ministry: Timothy & Titus," *Church* 3 (Summer 1987) 20-24.

89. The passage is, however, read on Tuesday of the twenty-fourth week of the year (Year I).

90. See *Lumen Gentium*, 11: "The family is, so to speak, the domestic church. In it parents should, by their word and example, be the first preachers of the faith to their children."

91. See my *Letters That Paul Did Not Write*, 166-167; Robert A. Wild, "The Warrior and the Prisoner: Some Reflections on Ephesians 6:10-20," *Catholic Biblical Quarterly* 46 (1984) 284-298.

92. Many translations render the Greek's *ho kainos anthrōpos* as "new man." The Greek has a gender-inclusive *anthrōpos* rather than the gender-exclusive *anēr*. In an attempt to avoid the sexist quality of "new man," many translations, including the NRSV and the RNAB, speak about a "new self." This translation clearly avoids the apparent "sexism" of the older translations. "Self," however, evoking the Freudian "ego," has an individualistic ring

which is not present in the biblical text. The biblical text makes a rather clear allusion to the story of creation.

93. One might note that household language has been introduced into the passage when the author calls those to whom it is addressed "beloved children" (Eph 5:1).

94. This is not to imply that spousal abuse is to be tolerated in the name of Christian forgiveness. Masochism is not a Christian virtue.

95. See "Interpretation of the Bible," IV, C, 3, which states: "Preachers should certainly avoid insisting in a one-sided way on the obligations incumbent upon believers. The biblical message must preserve its principal characteristic of being the good news of salvation freely offered by God."

96. See also 1 Pet 3:1. The first letter of Peter seems, in fact, to have arisen from Pauline circles similar to those from which Colossians and Ephesians have sprung.

97. Respectively Heb 11:8, 11-12, 17-19 and 1 John 3:1-12, 21-24.

98. Respect for the literary form of biblical translations intended for liturgical readings is specifically prescribed by *Comme le prévoit* (see par. 30).

99. Cf. "Interpretation of the Bible," I,A,4, which states, "According to Divino Afflante Spiritu, the search for the literal sense of Scripture is an essential task of exegesis and, in order to fulfill this task, it is necessary to determine the literary genre of texts (cf. Enchiridion biblicum 560), something which the historical-critical method helps to achieve.... The historical-critical method opens up to the modern reader a path to the meaning of the biblical text such as we have it today."

100. See my *Letters That Paul Did Not Write*, 163-165.

101. The expansions are sometime adventitious, as is, for example the reference to the fourth commandment in Eph 6:2-3. See my

"Obedience, Children and the Fourth Commandment—A New Testament Note," *Louvain Studies* 4 (1972-73) 157-173.

102. See also 1 Pet 2:18–3:7.

103. A better translation of the Greek *mysterion* than the New American Bible's "foreshadowing."

104. See, for example, John F. O'Grady, *Pillars of Paul's Gospel*, 137-138.

105. In Greek, Paul's text reads "Jew or Greek, slave or freeman, male and female." The distinctive "and" which links male and female is an obvious reference to Gen 1:27, "male and female he created them."

106. See, for example, "The Interpretation of the Bible," I, E, 2, which cites the importance accorded to Gal 3:28 in the feminist approach to biblical interpretation.

107. See the introduction to the *New Order of Readings*, par. 10, which cites *Presbyterorum ordinis*, 4, "The preaching of the word is necessary for the sacramental ministry. For the sacraments are sacraments of faith and faith has its origin and sustenance in the word."

108. The second part of the midrash (Rom 10:8-9) is, nonetheless, read as the beginning of a scriptural lection on the first Sunday of Lent (Year C) and in the ritual Mass for the Presentation of the Creed.

109. See my *Letters That Paul Did Not Write*, 190-194.

110. Fortunately the lectionary approved for use in the United States does not include the reading of the verses which follow, 1 Tim 2:9-13. This passage's directives on women's role in the liturgical assembly are difficult to grasp. The Canadian lectionary uses the discretion provided by Roman documents to omit 1 Tim 2:8, a directive for men (the gender specific *andras*, in Greek),

which virtually calls for the reading of the parallel passage on women.

111. On the doctrine of inspiration see chapter nine, "Inspiration," pages 317-355 of my *Introduction to the New Testament* (Garden City, NY: Doubleday, 1983) and "Inspiration" in the *New Jerome Biblical Commentary*, 1023-1033. Although "The Interpretation of the Bible in the Church," has a section on "The Meaning of Inspired Scripture," the document does not reflect on the nature of the charism of inspiration.

112. See the various essays in Jan Lambrecht and Raymond F. Collins, eds., *God and Human Suffering* (Louvain Theological and Pastoral Monographs 3. Louvain: Peeters, 1990—Grand Rapids, MI: Eerdmans, 1991). See, further, Charles H. Talbert, *Learning Through Suffering: The Education Value of Suffering in the New Testament* (Zacchaeus Studies: New Testament. Collegeville, MN: Liturgical, 1991).

113. Elisabeth Schüssler Fiorenza's *Jesus: Miriam's Child, Sophia's Prophet. Critical Issues in Feminist Christology* (New York: Continuum, 1994) points to some of the difficulties which can arise from an undue emphasis on the sufferings of Jesus. See, especially, chapter 4 (pp. 97-128).

114. In the United States the readings from the feast of Joseph the Worker may also be used on Labor Day, the first Monday of September.

115. See Matt 17:1-13; Mark 9:2-13.

116. A helpful summary of some of the principles pertinent to the preparation of a contemporary "liturgical text" is given in an editorial note of the *Canadian Bishops' Conference Lectionary: Sundays and Solemnities*, iii. The pertinent Roman documents are the *Order for the Readings of Mass* and *Comme le prévoit*, the January 25, 1969 Instruction of the Sacred Congregation for the Sacraments and Divine Worship on the translation of liturgical texts for celebrations with a congregation.

117. The New Revised Standard Version of the Bible (NRSV, 1990) was intended for use in public reading and congregational worship. See, in this regard, Bruce Metzger's preface to the version as well as Robert C. Dentan, "The Story of the New Revised Standard Version," in Bruce M. Metzger, Robert C. Dentan, Walter Harrelson, *The Making of the New Revised Standard Version of the Bible* (Grand Rapids: Eerdmans, 1991) 1-21.

118. The 1970 Catholic Book edition of the *Lectionary for Mass*, commonly used in the United States, took its readings from the original edition (1970) of the New American Bible. The revision of this lectionary will make use of the third revised edition of the New American Bible.

119. The same is true of the New English Bible, but this text, which is commonly used in Great Britain, is not widely read in the United States and has not been approved for liturgical use by the National Conference of Catholic Bishops.

120. See *Lectionary: Sundays and Solemnities*, iii.

121. See the introduction to the *New Order of Readings*, par. 124.

122. This is the phraseology of the Canadian lectionary, based on the New Revised Standard Version.

123. Our count includes only those instances in which "*adelphoi*—brothers and sisters" is used as a form of address. It should be added that, in some cases, Paul's use of the term has become so repetitious that some of the recent translations have made a stylistic substitution for one or another occurrence of the expression. For example, "Beloved (*adelphoi*), pray for us. Greet all the brothers and sisters (*adelphous*) with a holy kiss. I solemnly command you by the Lord that this letter be read to all of them (*adelphois*)" (1 Thess 5:25-27, NRSV).

124. The vocative form also occurs nine times in Galatians and three times in 2 Corinthians. In contrast, it is not at all used in the epistle to the Ephesians. Since Paul had stayed among the

Ephesians for about three years, its absence from this text is particularly notable. The absence is one of the reasons why scholars today generally doubt that it was the apostle himself who wrote this text.

125. See Matt 3:1.

126. This remark obviously also pertains to the subjects implied in the declined form of the Bible's original Hebrew or Greek texts.

127. When, for example, the passage about the stilling of the storm is read from the gospel according to Mark on the twelfth Sunday of Year B, it begins,"One day as evening drew on Jesus said to his disciples, 'Let us cross over to the farther shore.'" In the New American Bible, however, the passage reads:"That day as evening drew on he said to them, 'Let us cross over to the farther shore'" (Mark 4:35). The lectionary text has changed "that day" to "one day" and, for clarification's sake, it has added "Jesus" and "his disciples." The (Canadian) lectionary text, based on the New Revised Standard Version, has similarly added "Jesus" and "his disciples," but has dropped "on that day."

128. One of Paul's most earnest appeals,"Beware of the dogs! Beware of the evil-workers! Beware of the mutilation!" (Phil 3:2), is absent from the liturgy. The passage to which it appears is not read on Sunday; it is read on Thursday of the thirty-first week of the year (Year II), but even then verse 2 is not proclaimed to the congregation.

129. This omission is consistent with the absence of Rom 1:22-32 from the lectionary's choice of liturgical readings. See the discussion on p. 110.

130. "There is neither Jew nor Greek, there is neither slave nor free person, there is not male and female" is the translation offered by the New Revised Standard Version.

131. This is not the only instance of this liturgical phenomenon.

The same editorial modification, that is, the liturgical omission of the biblical text's explanatory *"gar*-for," is made when Philippians 3:3-8 is appropriated as a lection for Thursday of the thirty-first week in ordinary time (Year II).

132. In this instance the adversative particle is not the strong *"alla*-but," but the relatively weak *"de*-but." Interestingly, the exhortation to sanctify Christ as Lord, as part of the contrast experience (see 1 Pet 3:14-15), constitutes an exegetical problem for interpreters. The liturgical editing of the text has neatly eliminated the crux.

133. The text continues:"But there could be no justification for depriving the faithful of the spiritual riches of certain texts on the grounds of difficulty if its source is the inadequacy either of the religious education that every Christian should have or of the biblical formation that every pastor should have."

134. See the introduction to the *Lectionary for Mass*, 7. The text is reproduced in the introduction to the *New Order of Readings*, pars. 75-77.

135. Insofar as possible, my references to the scriptural chapters and verses in this chapter will be made on the basis of their use or non-use in the liturgy. Hence, they may not always conform to what might be considered the natural division of the biblical text. In this regard, see the previous chapter's discussion about the liturgy's removal of scriptural passages from their biblical context.

136. This occurrence is hardly by chance. It is specifically noted in the introduction to the *Lectionary for Mass*.

137. Cf. Joël Delobel, "Coherence and Relevance of 1 Cor 8-10," a paper delivered during the August 1994 Colloquium Biblicum Lovaniense, to be published by the Leuven University Press.

138. Neither of these contentious passages appears in the series of scriptural lections appointed for reading on weekdays.

139. It must be recognized that the first part of this exhortation presents serious exegetical problems for the interpreter, especially vv. 4-6, where the meaning of the Greek expressions rendered by the revised New American Bible respectively as "to acquire a wife" and "to take advantage of or to exploit ... in this matter" is a subject of scholarly debate. While, in my judgment, the revised NAB correctly conveys the meaning of Paul's words, the NAB translates the first expression as "guarding his member," almost as if Paul were urging sexual asceticism rather than counseling the Thessalonians to get married.

140. See the readings for the Tuesday and Wednesday of the twenty-seventh week of the year (Year II).

141. See, for example, the *Catechism of the Catholic Church*, par. 1852 and pars. 736, 1470, 1832, 2113.

142. See Phlm 1.

143. See S. Scott Bartchy, "Philemon, Epistle to," *Anchor Bible Dictionary*, 5, 305-310.

144. In the words of Vatican Council II, the canon of the New Testament contains, in addition to the four gospels, "the epistles of St. Paul and other apostolic writings" (*Dei Verbum*, 20).

145. For that matter, neither of these dramatic scenarios is reprised in the weekday lectionary.

146. See also the 19th Sunday in Year C, when Heb 11:1-2, 8-19 is read.

147. See Roman 3:28, a passage which is reprised on the ninth Sunday of the year (Year A). Although the New American Bible translated Paul's *erga nomou* as "observance of the law," the New Revised Standard Version and the revised NAB render the phrase according to its classic translation, "the works of the law."

148. By limiting its selection from Hebrews 11 of the recital of the

heroes of patriarchal times, the lectionary has also omitted Hebrews' citation of Rahab as an example of faith (Heb 11:31).

149. See H. Denziger and A. Schönmetzer, *Enchiridion symbolorum definitionum et declarationum de rebus fidei et morum* 1695, 1716, 1718-1719.

150. The intervenient hymnic material on the suffering Christ (1 Pet 2:21-25) has made its way into the lectionary, on the fourth Sunday of Easter (Year A).

151. See Rom 10:9.

Scripture Index

Liturgical and Feast Index

Year B	16, 21, 31, 34, 38-39, 43, 50-53, 59, 61
Easter Season	59, 122
2nd - 6th Sunday of the year	50, 113
4th - 6th Sunday of the year	51
5th Sunday of the year	112
7th - 14th Sunday of the year	50, 52, 117
7th Sunday of the year	53, 131
12th Sunday of the year	139
13th Sunday of the year	26, 53, 114
15th - 21st Sunday of the year	53
17th - 21st Sunday of the year	73
17th Sunday of the year	73-74
18th Sunday of the year	74-75, 105
19th Sunday of the year	75-76
20th Sunday of the year	76-78
21st Sunday of the year	78-85
22nd - 26th Sunday of the year	53
22nd Sunday of the year	105, 107
24th Sunday of the year	87
27th - 33rd Sunday of the year	53
Christ the King	64
Year C	16, 21, 34, 38-39, 43, 59
1st Sunday of Advent	70
1st Sunday of Lent	136
2nd Sunday of Lent	20
Easter Season	59, 63-65
2nd Sunday of Easter	60, 61
2nd - 8th Sunday of the year	54-55
2nd - 4th Sunday of the year	112
4th Sunday of the year	107
5th Sunday of the year	19
6th Sunday of the year	105
9th - 18th Sunday of the year	56, 116
10th - 14th Sunday of the year	57
12th Sunday of the year	86-88, 105-106
15th - 18th Sunday of the year	88-89